# THE
# Quality
# Management
# MANUAL

## HOW TO WRITE AND DEVELOP A SUCCESSFUL MANUAL FOR QUALITY MANAGEMENT SYSTEMS

Jenny Waller
Derek Allen
Andrew Burns

Kogan Page Ltd, London
Nichols Publishing Company,
New Jersey

First published in 1993

Kogan Page Limited
120 Pentonville Road
London N1 9JN

**British Library Cataloguing in Publication Data**
A CIP record for this book is available from the British Library.

ISBN 0 7494 0903 7

Published in the United States of America by Nichols Publishing,
P.O. Box 6036, East Brunswick, New Jersey 08816

ISBN (US) 0 89397 388 2

*Library of Congress Cataloging-in-Publication Data*
Waller, Jenny.
    The quality management manual : how to write and develop a
successful manual for quality management / Jenny Waller, Derek
Allen, and Andrew Burns.
        p.   cm.
    Includes index.
    ISBN 0-89397-388-2 : $49.95
    1. Total quality management—Handbooks, manuals, etc.   2. Quality
control—Handbooks, manuals, etc.   I. Allen, Derek, 1955–
II. Burns, Andrew, 1954–        III. Title.
HD82.15.W35   1993
658.5'62   dc20                                        93–5035
                                                        CIP

Typeset by Saxon Graphics Ltd, Derby
Printed and bound in Great Britain by Biddles Ltd, Guildford and Kings Lynn.

# Contents

# Acknowledgements

Thanks to everyone at IDU and CMC for their contributions to the content of this book, and for their help in writing it.

# Part 1 About the Quality Management Manual

# Introduction 1

This book *won't* provide you with a specimen quality management manual, an off-the-shelf package for you to adjust to your own needs. There are books that will attempt to do this; this definitely isn't one of them.

Instead this book shows you how to make sure that your quality management manual not only conforms to the ISO9000 quality management standard, but also:

▲ The quality management standard can be referred to as either:
BS5750 (the British standard)
ISO9000 (the international standard)
EN 29000 (the European standard).
There is no difference between these. Throughout this book we will refer to the standard as ISO9000 for simplicity.

- reflects a quality management system which is properly tailored to the needs of your organisation

- is clear and easy to use, and therefore likely to be used

- provides you with the flexibility to run your business and make money.

As you will see as you read on, preparing a quality management manual from first principles in this way is a demanding task which will take time and care to get right.

You may ask why you should take the long way round. Why don't we just give you a quality management manual which will tell you how you have to do things?

Well, experience shows that short cuts like this don't work: they won't get you where you want to go. If you try to write a quality management manual without going through the processes we describe, you'll end up with something which looks all right on paper, but which doesn't have much to do with the way your organisation works in practice. That means you'll lose out in two ways.

Firstly, if your purpose in developing a quality management manual is to improve the efficiency and effectiveness of your organisation, an off-the-shelf manual will fail, even if you do manage to implement it. It will probably just provide you with a system that turns into a bureaucratic nightmare, forcing you to do things that you don't want to do and that don't make sense.

Secondly, if you aim to achieve registration to the quality management standard ISO9000, an off-the-shelf manual may get you past the desktop audit, but it won't survive the assessment visit. Assessors are very sensitive to manuals which don't seem to relate to the organisations they are supposed to represent. And one of the most common reasons to fail assessment is for non-conformance, where the assessor finds instances where the manual describes a process one way and the staff carry it out another way. The chances of this happening with a manual which is an 'outside' product are really very high, for people, quite rightly, will not see much point in new procedures which aren't built around their experience of what is important.

Good quality management manuals are a very powerful tool in communicating and controlling quality management systems. They are worth getting right.

## Who this book is for

This book is primarily for anyone who is interested or involved in setting up a quality management system which conforms to the quality management standard ISO9000.

The book explains:

- the role of the quality management manual

- the kind of information that is in it

- how to go about finding and presenting the information that has to be there

- how to implement and develop the quality management manual.

Whether or not you are actually going to prepare the quality management manual yourself, this book will help you to see what is involved in preparing it and how to assess the completed manual.

Ten years ago, or even less, anyone interested or involved in setting up a quality management system would probably have been from a large organisation in a manufacturing industry sector. However that is no longer true. The rising numbers of companies seeking registration increasingly include small organ-isations, and quality management has moved on from manufac-turing. By going back to first principles, the advice given in this

◆ Service sector registrations are increasing. Solicitors, management consultants, schools, design studios and architects' practices are some of the service industries now achieving registration. In 1992 the Epping Breast Screening Unit gained ISO9000 registration.

book will apply to quality management manuals for all sizes of organisations and all industry sectors.

It is worth mentioning here that although this book assumes that you want to take your organisation right through to registration for ISO9000, you don't have to. It is perfectly possible to decide that you would gain from a quality management system and a quality management manual without undergoing the rigours and expense of actual registration. This might be true for very small organisations, perhaps a sole trader. It might also be true for organisations undergoing particularly far-reaching change programmes. The quality management manual could have a central role to play in controlling and defining the change programme, but the organisation might not be ready for the pressures of registration until the change programme has become established.

◆ Change pro-grammes where the quality management manual can play a central role are:
– computerisation
– moving offices
– downsizing
– expanding.

And finally, if you are part of a company which already has ISO9000 registration and a quality management manual, you should still read this book. After gaining ISO9000 registration, organisations need to make sure that they don't stand still and that there is a continuing drive towards higher levels of quality. The process of looking beyond the requirements of ISO9000 to the wider quality needs of the organisation is called Total Quality Management. As part of your Total Quality Management pro-gramme, perhaps you should look at your manual again. Maybe it could be better.

◆ Some ideas for improving your quality management manual could be:
– defining management processes more clearly
– reducing unnecessary paperwork
– replacing text with diagrams
– writing in plain English, not 'quality speak'.

## The role of the quality management manual

The quality management manual is effectively a written sum-mary of all the quality management activity in your organisation. It has two roles:

- as a symbol or icon representing your quality management system

■ See section 4.2 of ISO9001 (1987).

- as a practical reference book or guide to your quality manage-ment system.

### *The quality management manual as an icon*

As an icon, the manual is something tangible which you can hold in your hands as evidence that you have succeeded in formalising and controlling your management processes. This is the docu-ment that your quality management assessors will hold in *their* hands when you apply for registration. It will be seen as definitive, the complete guide to how your organisation operates.

### The quality management manual as a reference book

The information in the quality management manual will influence the way virtually everyone in your organisation carries out their tasks. So it isn't a public relations exercise, something to show to the chairman of the board on a visit. It is a working document which has to be relevant to the people who are expected to use it.

It is important to keep these two roles clear in your mind as you set about preparing the quality management manual. If you concentrate too much on the manual as an icon or symbol, you may get carried away and start to describe a theoretical dream-world where everything is logically defined and prescribed in an ideal way. Remember that the quality management manual must exactly reflect the way your quality management system works in practice. If it doesn't, your quality management assessor won't applaud your idealism: your organisation will fail the assessment. On the other hand, if you just see the quality management manual as a functional document which is there to make sure people know what to do, you will tend to underestimate its importance and fail to exploit its significance as an icon or unifying symbol of achievement. A good quality management manual will fulfil both roles by achieving a balance between them.

## The style of the quality management manual

From what we have said so far, it is clear that the quality management manual is an important document, the end product of a considerable investment of the organisation's time and money. But the evidence seems to be that the quality management manuals that are being produced, while factually correct, are often quite unsophisticated from the point of view of the outsider or user.

The reasons for this are probably historical (see Chapter 2, *A Brief History of Quality Management Manuals*). In the early days, a good old-fashioned manual would be typed, photocopied and stapled or strung together with tags. It would soon get folded and crumpled with use. It was a document which traditionally looked practical and functional and which didn't make any concessions to those outside the manufacturing culture it represented.

And surprisingly, in the age of desktop publishing (DTP) and word processors, many or even most quality management manuals look much the same today. This is often in contrast to the same organisation's training and employee communications literature which is likely to be professionally produced. Clearly the quality management manual isn't thought to rate the same treatment, although it is aimed at the same audience. Yet in its way the quality management manual has as much to say about the organisation as training materials. By presenting the quality manual poorly, you are signalling that it isn't of practical importance, beyond complying with the assessors' requirements.

Given the importance of the organisation's investment in quality, the manual, as the tangible evidence of this investment, should surely look as if it matters, as if it reflects the organisation's commitment to quality and its understanding of the customer's point of view – internal or external.

A good quality management manual is an important document for its users – and it needs to look that way. So instead of being a dry, technical and purely functional document put together cheaply, it should be friendly, attractive, accessible and stylish – something which brings out the importance of the user and his or her role in the organisation and moves the organisation forward in its understanding of its own quality goals. In other words, the quality management manual should be a quality product. It is unlikely in this day and age, when our expectations of the standard of printed materials are so high, that anything else will be taken seriously.

## Case study

### Rubber Mouldings Ltd – Finding a Business Philosophy

Rubber Mouldings Ltd was a traditional engineering manufacturing company making precision rubber mouldings for general engineering and high technology applications.

It was owned by the Gilchrist family and seemed to be very successful, at least successful enough to provide the Gilchrists with a very comfortable income and three top-of-the-range, prestige European cars parked outside their factory.

RML also seemed the ideal candidate for quality management certification. It had a very small management team, a well-established manufacturing technology and blue-chip clients who wanted consistent, tried-and-tested designs.

The Gilchrists had been asked by two of their larger customers to consider implementing ISO9000 and had decided to take this route. They had also decided to use consultants to run the project which, on the surface, looked quite straightforward.

When the consultants started work, RML seemed to them to be a typical manufacturing company. Behind the calm facade and the modest but comfortable offices was the shop floor, characterised by an air of activity, the smell of rubber, noise and heat. Facilities on the shop floor were basic, and no doubt white-collar workers used to air-conditioned offices, personal computers and restaurant lunches would have found its atmosphere positively Dickensian. But the signs of prosperity were there nevertheless, in new equipment, in quality control systems, in the piles of goods waiting to be delivered, and in the long list of blue-chip customers.

But RML was not what it seemed. Under the surface something was wrong. The business went on from day to day, producing the mouldings and collecting the cash. But there was virtually no management system underpinning it. The consultants found they couldn't just move in and write a quality management manual which reflected the management system, because the management system wasn't there.

Gordon Gilchrist had established the technical base of the business. His brother's wife Veronica helped him by doing the books in the evenings and at weekends and establishing a basic business system. Veronica believed in chasing payments and in controlling all expenditure: these beliefs were established as fundamentals of the business.

The business continued to grow. Gordon's brother Jack joined, and the family invested in two more machines. At this point decisions were made which shaped the company for the immediate future. Jack took on the role of buyer, governed by strict price parameters, and also the responsibility for machine maintenance. He had a very practical nature and always seemed to know how to get the best out of the machines if they were playing up.

Gordon took on the sales and estimating role – after all, customers were now used to dealing with him, and he did have a keen eye for the commercial side of the business.

He also adopted the quality control role. Because of his close links with the customers, he knew what he could get away with. His quality control system was simple – put the good ones into one pile and the bad ones into another pile. On a good day, the good ones were delivered and the bad ones reprocessed for commercial-grade rubber. On a bad day, however, when batches for the customers were short, a few of the bad ones would be reinspected and found not to be as bad as they had first seemed – they became good ones and the batch was made up to the necessary number.

Quality control was a fine balancing act which required a very wide range of skills. Gordon had to judge when he could afford to ignore the tolerances on a drawing, for example if the customers themselves were short of deliveries in that production period and would ignore the quality of something as small as a rubber moulding, and when the customer actually worked to drawing.

As cash allowed, the company grew. Veronica joined full-time as bookkeeper, secretary, administrator and 'girl Friday'. RML bought newer machines and a bigger factory unit, then brand new machines and brand new offices. With the expansion came employees and a part-time accountant, a nice chap recommended by the local Chamber of Commerce. He didn't know much about the rubber industry, or indeed any manufacturing industry. What he was employed to do was to check the books.

Veronica resented his occasional attempts to offer business advice:

> At the beginning he used to try to make us pay for fancy stuff
> like business plans, or marketing or strategic business advice. He
> soon stopped when we refused to pay his bills though. Now he
> just does what he's supposed to: checks the books.

When the consultants got to know the company ten years after it began, RML had over 50 staff, a multi-million pound turnover and an impressive range of machinery. They even had a quality control manager and an extensive quality control lab – purchased from a bankrupt subcontractor. Gordon explained this decision:

> I was forced into it really. We were after this big ministry contract, and we had to have the whole quality control works for it – you know how fussy these government purchasing departments are. Anyway the QC manager is useful in his way: he does a lot of the sorting and drives the van. He's also good when we show people round. He doesn't know how to operate all the inspection machinery yet because we can't find the time for him to train, and anyway it's a bit costly too: over £200 for a 2-day course! Anyway as things are he keeps the customers happy, and that's what it's all about at the end of the day, isn't it?

RML were confident that their quality control manager would be the key to ISO9000 registration. And they had definitely decided to register:

> Well, not so much wanted to as forced to really. Like the quality control thing – we need to keep it up and to impress the customers. Can't see the point myself, but the DTI scheme will pay for 50% of your fees – so why not?

It was at this point that the consultants discovered that RML were running their multi-million pound business without a management structure. There was no management team, no marketing plan, no business plan – just the three Gilchrists and the QC manager, whose work was very often re-done by Gordon Gilchrist anyway. Previous attempts at delegation had been disastrous. A bookkeeper had been appointed, but didn't do things correctly and left. A typist had been appointed, but she was sacked because she didn't pull her weight. The business survived in a seat-of-the-pants, crisis-management sort of way. The Gilchrists never took a holiday and were regularly working 12 hours a day.

RML didn't just need a quality management manual – they needed a management system. And because after ten years of driving the business through sheer will-power the Gilchrists were running out of energy, they were prepared to listen to the consultants and to start to do something about it.

The decision was as much a personal as a business decision. The Gilchrists had to re-examine why they were in business and what they wanted from it. They had two alternatives: either they could continue to do everything themselves, or they could install some management. They chose the latter.

Throughout the quality management project the principles and practice of management were introduced to the Gilchrists almost without them being aware of it. Issues to do with things like planning, leadership, delegation, responsibility and authority, organisation, control, management style and motivation were discussed in the context of their own experiences as successful entrepreneurs. The project became a journey of exploration and learning. Some ideas were accepted, others rejected. But most importantly, the family came to understand what they wanted from their business and how they could set about achieving it.

They were just in time, for shortly afterwards the defence industry, on which they depended, began to collapse. The quality management system had provided the catalyst to help manage the change necessary for survival. The procedures reduced the need for crisis management and allowed the directors to spend their time in planning and directing the business. Slowly the previously rudderless ship turned into an organisation in control of its own destiny and able to respond to the pressures of change.

Writing a quality management manual isn't just about applying techniques: it is about analysing and evaluating every aspect of your organisation's management. RML learned that the hard way and survived. Many companies haven't.

# A Brief History of Quality Management Manuals 2

## Quality management manuals in the UK today

Quality management manuals abound in UK organisations these days. There are now nearly 20,000 companies registered with ISO9000 and by 1994 it is estimated that there will be double this number. In the UK, the BS5750 registered firms logo is becoming increasingly familiar as it flashes past on lorries on the motorway and adorns stationery and product catalogues. Such is the momentum of the initiative, indeed, that the question among business colleagues now is why you aren't registered yet and when you plan to be, not whether or not you've heard of the standard, as was the case just a few years ago.

Add to the numbers of registered companies the organisations who have not yet achieved registration to the standard, or who have decided for one reason or another not to pursue registration but who have developed their own version of a quality management manual, and you have quite a phenomenon to consider.

You will have also quite a number of questions to ask:

- Why this sudden interest in quality management systems?

- What are other countries doing about quality – Japan, the US, Europe?

- Why ISO9000?

- What are the benefits?

- What are the drawbacks?

And then there is the biggest question of all:

- How do I make this initiative work for my organisation – how can I make ISO9000 add value to what my organisation does?

# Why quality management systems anyway?

◆ 90% of British industry is still made up of companies employing less than 10 people. The BSi is currently looking into the possibility of developing a small business version of ISO9000. Sole traders have been registered under the standard as it is now, but BSi admits that small business needs may not be catered for fully.

This is a very interesting question, particularly when you consider that even in the 1990s, when multinationals are well-established in the UK, British industry is still mostly made up of small companies, among whom there is no deep-seated tradition of formal management systems.

On the contrary, the British owner-manager has always had the reputation of being something of an incurable amateur, while management training seems to focus on the needs of the large multinationals. This point is well illustrated by the case study at the end of Chapter 1, which describes a typical example of the British approach based on common sense and prudence.

Adopting ISO9000 represents quite a challenge for these companies, based as it is on unfamiliar concepts such as:

- creating management structures

- defining requirements

- agreeing and formalising procedures

- taking corrective action

- carrying out internal audits.

The whole process of formalising procedures, writing the quality management manual, persuading everyone to adopt the procedures and submitting to external assessment is clearly no picnic. The anecdotal vocabulary of preparing for and gaining registration to ISO9000 is dominated by words such as 'rigorous', 'demanding', 'hard slog' and 'expensive'.

So why do it?

The underlying answer lies in the current perception that *something* has to be done about quality in order to survive. Every owner or director in the 1990s must work out for themselves whether this perception is myth or reality.

## *Doing something about quality*

The reason for the current obsession with quality can be summed up in one word: Japan. Post-war Japan produced nothing of quality. Japan was generally regarded as a purveyor of cheap and shoddy goods to the international community in any sector you cared to choose. Perhaps some of you will remember seeing your first Japanese portable radio or motorcycle. Such products hardly seemed to pose a threat to the might of the Western industrial economies. Customers only bought Japanese goods because they were cheap and cheerful. In fact Japan's quality problems were so severe that the US exported free advice as part of Japan's post-war rehabilitation programme.

And then suddenly it wasn't true any more. Japanese products began to get a little better – not substantially so, but recognisably. And then a little better still. Until suddenly Japanese goods were of equal quality to Western goods, though generally cheaper.

Then Japanese goods were significantly better: more innovative, more exciting, better designed, better distributed and more reliable. Until finally there were no Western goods for comparison in an alarming number of sectors: electronics, motorcycles, cameras and textiles, to name but a few.

International awareness slowly came to terms with the fact that this had not happened just because the Japanese had a comparative price advantage, or a more dedicated workforce, or luck. The answer lay in quality: each product cycle was just a little bit better than the one before. The Japanese had steadily improved their management and their products until they could achieve levels of quality in design, manufacture, cost control and marketing which were higher than those in the West. It was time for Western businesses to think again about what quality meant, and to face the reality of quality guru Deming's famous statement:

> You don't have to do any of these things: survival isn't compulsory.

British companies still in business after the Japanese quality revolution needed quality things to do.

## Quality initiatives abroad

Since the drive to improve quality is international, it is interesting to consider how quality is understood and put into practice in countries outside the UK.

### Japan

The obvious place to start is Japan. Ironically, it was the work of two Americans, Juran and Deming, which was instrumental in introducing to Japan concepts which were to take quality well beyond the idea of shop-floor inspection to quality as something strategic, which would influence decision making throughout the organisation.

Juran's interest in quality started in his role as a statistician at General Electric. His background in statistical methods is

▲ The understanding of quality as the inspection process which takes place just before the customer receives the goods or services is known as *quality control*.
The concept of quality as something which drives the work of the organisation from beginning to end is known as *quality assurance*.

▲ Pareto analysis states that the vital few, or the 20 per cent, account for 80 per cent of the cost or value, or number of complaints, or any other measurement, rather than the trivial many which account for just 20 per cent of the cost, or value, or number of complaints, or any other measure.

reflected in his enthusiasm for the ever-present principle of Pareto analysis, for example.

Juran went on to relate quality objectives to business objectives by introducing the concept of quality as *fitness for purpose*. According to this definition a quality product was not just the most expensive one: it was the product which fulfilled the purpose the customer had for it. So, while a Rolls Royce was obviously a quality car, a Mini could also be a quality car, since it fulfilled the purpose of providing a cheap, reliable and economical means of transport for the family (and perhaps a little luggage). This concept of quality was much more searching than any previous definition as conformance to specification: it meant looking at why products were made as well as how, thus introducing quality as a strategic issue which put customers and customers' needs right at the centre of the business.

Deming, like Juran, had worked as a statistician for General Electric. He too had a solid background in what is known as scientific management, or management by numerical analysis. Deming formulated his own set of management methods and tools designed to collect data on 'characteristics' and to institute problem-solving tools and systems for communication and feedback. He also identified key roles for a quality management system and the team and cultural conditions necessary to succeed. Deming found post-war Japanese industry receptive to his ideas and willing to invest the time and effort needed to implement properly the techniques he advocated – techniques such as statistical analysis and control charts.

### The United States of America

Unlike Japan, the US had really no reason in the post-war period to take the issue of quality very seriously. In the military and aeorospace industries quality was controlled by an extensive range of statistically-based quality techniques, some of which had filtered through to general industry.

After all, US goods were the best in the world. As the world economy struggled to start again, consumers couldn't get enough of them. There was no need to pay close attention to Deming and Juran, or to struggle to take on board the disciplines they advocated.

This situation held until the Japanese quality revolution. It was in this context that the work of Philip Crosby began to ring true. Crosby, previously quality director of ITT, had a quality message that appealed directly to the boardrooms of increasingly beleaguered US corporations. Crosby linked quality to cost. He

◆ Crosby identified two types of quality costs:
The cost of conformance – getting it right first time.
The cost of non-conformance – getting it wrong, and having to put it right.

called his first book *Quality is Free* (McGraw Hill, 1978) arguing that an optimal investment in quality practices throughout an organisation would, by cutting re-work costs, effectively be free. His book became an immediate bestseller in the US, probably because it talked the language of the major corporations and their boardrooms – money.

Once quality had become a boardroom issue, the question remained of how to effect the cultural changes that were necessary to put in place good quality practices. After all, the US had the philosophy – now they needed to practise it. But the US workforce did not prove as compliant as its Japanese counterpart. The US quality drive of the 1980s took on an increasingly evangelistic tone as gurus such as Tom Peters or Earnest Huge preached the importance of commitment and cultural change in organisations.

In 1987, the Malcolm Baldridge National Quality Improvement Act established an annual United States National Quality award. The criteria for the award reflect the US understanding of quality issues by taking a considerably wider focus than ISO9000, incorporating 'softer' quality thinking as well as the 'harder' quality issues of statistical control and conformance.

◆ Tom Peters coined the phrase *Management by Walking About*, and Earnest Huge the expression *Walk the Talk*, to sum up the new involvement management needed to show to bring about changes in attitudes to quality.

◆ The Malcolm Baldridge Award examines seven areas:
- leadership
- the quality of information and analysis
- quality planning
- human resource utilisation
- quality assurance of products and services
- quality results
- customer satisfaction.

### Europe

Mainland Europe has faced the same international pressures to compete as the US or the UK so, not surprisingly, the debate about quality is lively there too. Indeed the quality culture in some European countries, notably Germany and Sweden, has always been very strong.

ISO9000 is now recognised throughout Europe as EN29000, and there are signs that the single European market is beginning to exert a harmonising influence. Registration to ISO9000/EN29000 could be the key to doing business in the Europe of the future. And there are definite signs that organisations in Eastern Europe are willing to adopt the standard, as a way to manage the ultimate change from communism to capitalism.

As well as the European standard, there is now also a European Quality Award (EQA) which has been set up to give recognition to companies who can demonstrate good quality practices.

◆ The number of registrations in Europe is still limited. In 1992 the figure for ISO9000 registrations was:
Norway – 17
Austria – 17
Germany – 240
France – 480.
However there are signs of an increasing interest in registering to the standard.

# Why ISO9000?

### Sector schemes

So why has the quality management standard ISO9000 been so successful in the UK? What is it about the standard that has persuaded so many companies to follow the registration route?

◆ Probably the best-known example of sector schemes, and one which is still in use, is the Ministry of Defence set of standards known as the AQAP (Allied Quality Assurance Publications) series. These control the manufacturing and testing of military products. However, they are now being replaced by ISO9000 in many companies.

Part of the answer is undoubtedly that the concept of using formalised procedures to control quality is not actually new in the UK: it has its origins in the sector schemes of the post-war period. These were developed by industries who relied on subcontractors to supply products which had to be safe and compatible with each other. The best way to ensure this was for the purchaser of the subcontracted work to issue mandatory standards and specifications to suppliers. Subcontractors would be visited and assessed for conformance to the sector scheme requirements, and their contracts taken away if they failed. This simple but effective enforcement technique gave the sector schemes enormous influence in their respective industries.

Sector schemes operated in public sector industries, for example the Ministry of Defence, the Post Office, London Transport and electricity and gas. Others were developed by the private sector in industries such as aerospace and oil. If you wanted to work for these organisations, then you had to have a standards manual and be able to show conformance to the sector scheme guidelines.

Sector schemes were essentially about conformance. They were about following instructions to the letter, about relying on procedures to ensure a high quality of product. They were also geared entirely to production and manufacturing, and to stable processes where change was not anticipated.

### BS5750

■ See Foreword to BS5750 Part 1 (1979)

In 1979 the British Standards Institute (BSi) published its first quality management standard, BS5750. This was based very closely on the Ministry of Defence 05 series of standards (later to become the AQAP series) with which British manufacturing industry had become familiar, and was chiefly designed for production companies, tending to concentrate on inspection and quality control issues.

There was in fact a debate within the BSi at this time about whether or not to include the word *quality* in the title of the standard. The word did appear, of course, but the BSi estimates that this decision slowed down the uptake of the standard by five years, such was the lowly status of quality at that time.

But times change. Developments in international thinking about quality began to filter through to the UK. Influential books and training courses from the quality gurus appeared on the market and as British products disappeared from the shops, there was at last a realisation of the strategic importance of quality management to business survival.

This increase in awareness resulted firstly in an increased uptake of BS5750, and then in pressure on the standard to move away from the original prescriptiveness of its approach to a more flexible framework which would allow organisations to develop their own policies and procedures, and which could be adapted to service organisations. In 1987 BSi responded with an updated standard, supplemented by simplified interpretations of the standard specific to various industry sectors. It is this set of standards which is now accepted as the international standard ISO9000 and which has such influence today, providing a practical action plan for managers who want to do something about quality, but who would otherwise quickly become lost in the intangibles and vagaries of many of the messages from today's quality gurus.

## The benefits of ISO9000

The disciplines established by the quality management standard are clearly important, forcing organisations to think through how they operate and to keep control of what they do. And indeed in a sector like the military, where the sector schemes began, it is obviously reassuring to know that all the engineering processes involved in producing our weaponry have been tightly controlled.

The present-day, post-Chernobyl concern with the quality and safety of nuclear installations makes this point very well. We the public want to know that everything is under control. And how better to show this than to point to quality management manuals which set the standard for conformance in all activities in the nuclear plant?

▲ All nuclear power plants are required by law to meet certain safety standards. There is also a British Standard for owners of nuclear facilities, which requires management control procedures to meet 18 specific criteria.

In November 1989, Sellafield atomic power station was able to tell *Quality Assurance News* magazine that by the end of the year there would be manuals for each organisation, department and plant – over 50 in all. This greatly increases the visibility of Sellafield's operations and inspires public confidence, especially as the introduction of the manuals will be supported by a full audit programme. We can see above all that Sellafield is taking quality seriously.

## Some limitations of ISO9000

However, there can be limitations to the quality management standard, particularly if it is used prescriptively, in a similar way to the sector schemes. And we must remember that the sector schemes didn't actually achieve their objectives. Only recently there have been questions in Parliament concerning the escalation of military costs owing to unplanned maintenance and equipment failure – hardly the result of a quality system that has worked.

The problem with sector schemes in particular, and with prescriptive quality management schemes in general, is that they limit concepts of quality to checking and conformance, or quality control. That doesn't deliver quality assurance. We can give three examples of what can go wrong.

Consider firstly a small engineering company which was totally dependent on a government agency which required strict compliance to all its instructions and specifications. The company was a valued supplier and had built up a good reputation for supplying quality goods. However, one product that they were asked to supply seemed to them to have been wrongly specified. Not only was it extremely difficult to maintain the required tolerances, but it was also felt that they were probably unnecessary anyway. When the company queried this, they were told that it was not their responsibility to question their instructions, but to perform the work exactly to the specification. When the products were supplied, batch after batch were rejected. The company was told that their competitors' products weren't faulty and therefore they should rework the batches free of charge. It was not until some months later that they realised that not only their own batches but also those of their competitors were being returned.

By the end of the contract, the small supplier went bankrupt. The specification was eventually changed, but it was too late for the company in question, who are now suing for restitution.

This is the first main problem with a conformance-based approach: quality in many cases does not mean conformance – it means questioning.

Consider secondly an article, 'Military Standard 105D: its uses and misuse', published by the Journal of the Institute of Quality Assurance. Military standard 105D is extensively used in industry for acceptance sampling. In the article two highly qualified and experienced quality managers discuss the problems people have with interpreting its requirements. In their introduction, they state that:

> while it is more important for operators who are directly
> involved in carrying out the inspection process to have a clear,
> basic understanding of the instructions for implementing the
> plan, rather than knowledge of the statistical principles behind it,
> engineers and higher management staff must have a certain

amount of statistical knowledge to decide on a plan with the required level of quality protection, as well as optimum cost-effectiveness. Ignoring this vital component has often resulted in misuse of the plan.

This is the second main problem with a conformance-based approach: people have to understand what they are doing to do it well.

Finally, consider the large ring-binder company with ISO9000 registration which is currently taking one of its customers to court. The company managed to deliver 2000 ring-binders which were the wrong size. In addition, over 20 per cent wouldn't close. When the customer pointed this out, and declined to pay, the company's reaction was to take its customer to court.

This shows two more problems with ISO9000, applied unthinkingly. The standard won't have anything to say about the standard of your product ('guaranteeing consistent rubbish', as one disillusioned businessman put it), or about your bad judgement. It won't stop you going out of business.

## Making ISO9000 work for you

The lessons from all this are clear enough. If you are going to make quality work for you, you must move right away from the concept of the quality management standard as a handy set of rules which you can apply indiscriminately to your organisation and which will solve all your problems.

On the contrary, you must see the standard only as a framework, a way of analysing and improving how your organisation manages itself.

This brings us back to quality management manuals. Sector scheme manuals were off-the-shelf books of rules. They didn't always work. If your quality management manual is going to work, it has to be a good deal more than that.

## The Construction Industry

The construction industry has traditionally had something of a cowboy reputation: seasonal working means that large contractors rely on using smaller subcontractors to flex capacity. The smaller subcontractors have to manage their own capacity and subcontract in turn. This leads to great difficulties in the management chain.

Even if the larger contractors keep their house in order, they can quickly lose control down the subcontracting chain. This leads to the problems which give the industry its reputation for things like delays in construction, as the subcontractors try to do too many jobs at once, escalating costs, owing to the delays, and even contractors disappearing.

Gradually, however, the construction industry has been losing its cowboy reputation. This is partly because of the controls brought in by legislation, such as improvements in Health and Safety, and COSHH. It is also due to the introduction of ISO9000 quality management standards.

ISO9000 is particularly appropriate for the construction industry because of its insistence on the control of subcontractors. Suppose one of the major players in construction adopts the quality management standard. This company can now specify that it will give preference to subcontractors who have also adopted the quality management standard. In times of recession, when every subcontractor is looking for a competitive edge, the compulsion for small subcontractors to put their management houses in order is very strong.

Because the move to adopt quality management systems is being driven by the largest contractors, many of these systems have taken on the characteristics of the earlier sector schemes and are bureaucratic and rather unthinking in their nature. So the problem of lack of management has been replaced by too many meaningless controls. This leads to situations where the quality management system results in less than a quality service to both internal and external customers:

- 'I can't process the order because ISO9000 won't let me.'
- 'I can't process the estimate because ISO9000 requires three signatures and you've only got two.'
- 'I can't order materials without the approval of a director.'

These situations arise when the purpose of the standard hasn't been understood. Competitive pressure will gradually force companies with such systems to rethink what they are supposed to achieve, and to remove their self-imposed shackles.

In many other ways the construction industry is well placed to improve its quality. It has a well-regulated training structure with technical apprenticeships and on-the-job training, so that there is a high level of specialist skills to draw from.

Smaller subcontractors are now under pressure to adopt the quality management standard. Their problem is to interpret the standard in a way which makes sense for the kind of businesses they run. Clearly the bureaucratic models of the larger contractors are not appropriate for outfits where the functions of marketing, sales, recruitment, staff appraisal, delegation, organisation structure or finance are hard to find, let alone control and develop. In these sorts of businesses, quality management will be a very searching process. It will force outfits which survive from season to season and from year to year on whatever fate brings, to address fundamental questions like 'Why am I in business?'

The construction industry represents an interesting case study in the development of ISO9000. Ultimately, initiatives from both ends of the industry will meet at some point in the future to produce appropriate and flexible models which can be combined throughout the subcontractor chain and include all sizes of contractors in their scope.

# The computer industry

The computer hardware sales and software development industries have shown an increasing awareness of customer needs over the last few years. In the early days of the industry, customers were presented with an impressive array of black boxes and software packages to choose from. Since the technology was new, customers had to rely on salespeople and, as a result, often ended up with equipment they didn't want and software they couldn't use.

Take the typical small computer hardware sales company, for example. These are very often set up by well-trained, aggressive and successful salespeople from one of the large multi-nationals. Taking their contacts and their ability to sell, they set up competitive outfits and start bringing in the orders.

But in the excitement of the selling, the routine, backroom activities such as processing the order, purchasing supplies or supplying support and maintenance tend to get forgotten. They simply aren't interesting to the entrepreneur, and they're only done when complaints from customers or the VAT man become too loud to ignore.

However, these companies are now beginning to feel pressure from increasingly knowledgeable and discerning customers to supply more than just a black box. Customers want solutions to their problems and customer care, rather than technical wizardry.

This has resulted in some interest in ISO9000 as a way of convincing customers of the efficiency and reliability of the company concerned. The culture clashes which result from introducing quality management procedures can be quite spectacular. But the fact remains that if a computer hardware sales company wants to move on from just shifting boxes, then the real needs of the customer will have to be addressed.

The software development sector of the computer industry is also under pressure to react more to customers' needs. Small software houses are very often started by talented young programmers who manage to sell a package to a major software house and suddenly find themselves with a significant user base and a turnover of millions of pounds. The company then grows by attracting more talented and creative program developers who don't like the constraints of working for large organisations and who are happiest working on their own, probably from home. The real excitement of the job is in dreaming up the next successful software package which will solve a technical problem, or a business problem, or become a popular computer game.

Routine development work for customers which requires the application of the constraints of agreed methodologies, test routines and software documentation, seems tedious by comparison. The only management these companies can agree to is a financial controller who counts the money as it rolls in and advises on investments. And this situation probably won't change until the money runs out. Without financial pressure, fulfilling customers' requirements on time and to budget will probably continue to come well down the list of priorities.

Yet every industry matures over time, and there are signs that software development houses who want a long-term future are beginning to take customer satisfaction much more seriously. The larger and more successful computer companies now advertise their products as computer solutions, rather than as specific items of hardware or software.

There is even an adaptation of the ISO9000 quality management standard, called the TickIT scheme, to help them.

## Case Study (i)

### Systemslink – Quality is Customer Service

Systemslink was a large multinational computer company. Its maintenance operation, employing nearly 1000 people in 14 locations, decided to go for registration to ISO9000. A quality management consultant, Dick Troughton, was duly appointed from one of the larger management consultancies and a date set to begin the project.

As part of the planning stage for implementing a quality management system, Dick always liked to get a good feel for the organisation he was working with. In this case, Dick thought that a day out on the road with the maintenance engineers would be a good introduction to the company and would tell him all that he needed to know. And he wasn't wrong.

Dick met up with Terry Jones bright and early, ready to take the first call that came in. Terry was dressed in yellow overalls with a blue logo on the breast pocket, and looked smart and efficient. Dick was impressed.

The first call came through at 9.10 from a solicitor's office in Harrogate. One of their PCs had gone down and needed to be repaired urgently, as the office was grinding to a halt without it. Terry explained confidently to Dick that this was a routine kind of call that he dealt with all the time, that he knew the system, and that they would be back in the office by lunch.

As he talked to Dick, Terry was walking down to the stores department. 'Need a kit of parts,' he explained, 'spares for the system. Standard issue. Every system has its own, so we can have everything we're going to need with us when we go out there.'

Once again, Dick was impressed. This was exactly the sort of idea he was used to being paid thousands of pounds to suggest. Terry put in his request at the stores department desk. Then the men waited. And waited. Eventually a rather flustered stores clerk came back clutching Terry's request slip.

'I'm sorry love,' she said to Terry, 'we haven't got any of them left at the moment. We've got an order in at the depot but delivery's not until Wednesday.'

Terry didn't seem too concerned. He explained to Dick that he had some common spares in the van and with any luck he wouldn't need the specialised kit of parts anyway. It was probably just a fuse or something similar which he could repair easily.

Unfortunately, however, Terry's preliminary diagnostic check showed that he did indeed need the kit of parts. The PC would need a new printed circuit board. This was specific to the make and model of the PC. Looking slightly embarrassed, Terry asked if he could use the phone and phoned the stores depot to arrange to have a kit biked over by courier.

As Terry made his arrangements, Dick was becoming increasingly sensitive to the atmosphere in the office. Although the staff were using their initiative and reverting wherever possible to manual systems, there were clearly a lot of tasks that couldn't be processed with the computer down and tension was building.

So when Terry politely explained that there would be a delay until the part arrived, it seemed like a good moment to show some sensitivity and slip away to lunch.

After lunch the courier arrived with the precious package and Terry quickly got to work. Thirty seconds later Dick heard a stifled expletive from behind the machine. Terry's head emerged. He looked a little wild. 'It's not here', he mouthed.

Dick was only grateful that Terry still had enough self-control left to speak quietly. But without a mobile phone he couldn't be as discreet as he could have wished. Asking for permission to use the phone once again, he had the feeling that the whole office was listening in as he reordered the kit, with special instructions to check for the circuit board before it left. Meanwhile it seemed like a good time to go for afternoon tea, as the temperature in the office was somehow becoming uncomfortably high.

Over tea, Dick reflected on the day's events so far. He had certainly learned a lot about what went on behind the smart head offices and training centres of Systemslink. Never mind the logo and the corporate identity, the uniforms and the modern blue service vans. Six hours after placing their call for emergency assistance, the solicitor's office was still not up and running again. And it didn't take much imagination to guess at what people's opinions of the company were going to be after this.

The second courier brought the right spares and in just a few minutes Terry succeeded in replacing the old board. Perspiring with relief, he sat down at the machine and began to boot up. Annoyingly, the system crashed. After the tenth crash, Terry gave up. Time to try something else.

This time nothing showed from the routine diagnostic tests. Everything should in theory have been working perfectly, but it wasn't. Terry admitted defeat. A senior engineer would have to sort this one out tomorrow. Meanwhile it was time for Dick and Terry to retreat as diplomatically as they could. The atmosphere in the van on the way back to Systemslink was somewhat bleak. Terry didn't need Dick to rub in the implications of what had gone wrong – a complete waste of resources, resulting in an upset client and a seriously tarnished image for the company.

Dick didn't have the courage to go back to the solicitor's office the next day, but he made sure to have a quiet word with the senior engineer when he returned. 'No problem,' reported the engineer. Sorted it out in five minutes. I keep telling the boys, you've got to check your software. Terry there was loading an old version – everyone's on version three these days.'

Dick had mixed feelings as he set about preparing his initial audit report. On the one hand, he wasn't looking forward to this job. It looked as if it could be pretty messy. On the other hand, wasn't this exactly what quality management systems were for? Accepting the discipline of the ISO9000 standard would have meant Terry getting the right kit in the right place at the right time. And a formal checklist would have forced Terry to check out the software version he was using. Systemslink would have had a satisfied customer to record, instead of one feeling frustrated and annoyed.

## Case Study (ii)
### The Mayfield Corporation – Quality Means Self-awareness

Mayfield were well on the way to ISO9000 registration. The system design had gone well – very well indeed. All the important policy decisions had been taken quickly and decisively by the directors and senior managers. The procedures were being drafted by project teams who were well on target. In fact, everything was going to plan.

Mayfield were particularly motivated to achieve registration as soon as possible, since their major competitor had achieved registration three months earlier and were aggressively pro-moting their success. They had set themselves the target of achieving Part 2 registration in three months, and Part 1 in six months. These were challenging targets, but achievable.

With the system design phase over, all that remained was to implement the system. But this is a dangerous part of any quality management project, known among consultants as 'death valley' because of all the remains of failed projects which lie scattered about the barren landscape. It isn't easy to survive death valley.

The key things to achieve are:

- *transfer of ownership*. It is the individual members of the organisation who will be assessed, not the project team.

- *instilling learning*. Everyone in the organisation needs to understand what is required.

- *action*. In death valley, no action takes place. Action means making it happen, correcting what's wrong, working to the procedure or working to have the procedure changed.

Mayfield decided that the way through death valley was to train a large number of staff, including senior management, in audit techniques. This would heighten awareness of the need for conformance throughout the company and ensure support for implementation at the very highest level.

As part of the audit training, a live audit was undertaken. This audit was to look at a particular contract worth £1 million which was going through the company at the time. The MD and the sales director were given the contract file for assessment. Using checklists and basic audit techniques, they were asked to audit the documentation for the project.

The results were spectacular. The MD and the sales director discovered that there was, in their own words, 'minimal control of the contract'. The most significant control mechanism they could find was a sheet of A3 paper with some scribbled notations. All the rest of the project control information was in the project manager's head.

The MD had recognised that in recent years the company's management processes had become rather ineffective. This was one reason for wanting to undertake ISO9000 registration. But even so he was shocked by what the audit revealed. It was as if all the taunts made by his competitors were true – and that really hurt. The day of the audit became known as Black Friday throughout the company, a phrase that accurately represented the MD's mood.

But by Monday, it became apparent that the shock of the audit had provided the impetus needed to get through death valley stage in record time. From the MD down, there was a determination to change things for the better and to do it quickly. So registration to both Parts 1 and 2 was achieved on target. Taking the audit route had provided the company with the impetus it needed to shake off its old practices and move forward.

# Part 2 The Content of the Quality Management Manual

# Definitions 3

## The quality management system

To understand the organising principles behind the quality management manual, you need to think about the structure of quality management systems.

Figure 1 shows how a typical quality management system works in an organisation. There can be variations of the model, of course – you may have more than three levels, or less. But for consistency we will use the three-level model throughout the book.

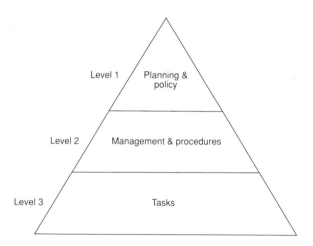

**Figure 1** *The quality management system triangle*

### *Level 1*

At the top of the organisation, at level 1, is senior management. This is the planning and policy-making level of the organisation where strategic decisions are made – about its direction, its purpose, and its culture. It is here that the decision to put the quality management system in place will be made.

### Level 2

In the middle of the organisation is the operational management level. Here people manage the implementation of the organisation's policies formulated at level 1. These people form a key group in any quality management system, because they are the ones who are going to interpret quality policies and develop workable procedures for everyone to follow.

### Level 3

At the base is the workforce, the people who follow the procedures which make up the policies and who represent the productive capability of the organisation. At this level there will be a particular concern with quality control issues and with checking what goes out of the door.

### Linking the levels

◆ The financial management system establishes records of things like:
– invoices
– purchase orders
– expenses claims.
The quality management system establishes records of things like:
– quotations
– orders
– purchase decisions.

The three levels of the quality management system are linked together by quality records and the auditing process. Just as a financial management system establishes records of key events, so the quality management system establishes records of the remaining key transactions in the business. And like the financial system, which is examined by a yearly audit, the quality management system is held together by an internal and external audit process.

## The quality management manual

▲ The quality policy manual is commonly referred to as the *quality manual.*

Documentation for the quality management system divides into three parts which reflect the three levels of the quality management system (see Figure 2).

There is often some confusion about the various terms used to describe the parts and the whole of the quality management manual. This confusion arises in the first place because the manual and its parts have similar-sounding names. And to make matters worse, the parts may actually be physically separated, if the organisation and its quality management system is large enough. As a result terms tend be used interchangeably; for example, people who are referring to what is strictly speaking a *quality policy manual* will probably call it, quite understandably, the *quality manual*. Of course this probably won't matter to most of the people most of the time, but if you do need to refer to one specific part of the manual, take care to emphasise exactly which part of it you mean.

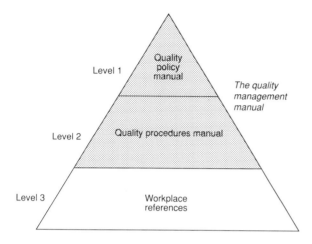

**Figure 2** *Documentation for the quality management system*

Here are the definitions we use.

## The quality management manual

We use the term *quality management manual* as a generic term. The quality management manual usually contains the documentation for the first two levels of the quality management system, and a guide to workplace references.

## Level 1: The quality policy manual

We refer to the first part of the quality management manual as the *quality policy manual*. This covers all the quality policies and plans coming from the top level of the organisation.

## Level 2: The quality procedures manual

We call the second part of the quality management manual the *quality procedures manual*, as it covers all the procedures which are developed and implemented at the middle level of the organisation.

▲ The quality procedures manual is often called the operations manual or management procedures.

▲ You may come across a number of ways of describing level 3 documentation, such as:
– workplace instructions
– third-level documentation
– work instructions
– support documentation.
We've chosen to call them workplace references.

Workplace references can include standard reference manuals, work instructions, technical manuals, codes of conduct, national and international standards and so on. The quantity of documents at this level can be quite large.

**Figure 3:** *Developing the quality management system and the quality management manual*

## Level 3: Workplace references

In addition to the quality management manual, most quality management systems involve reference materials, consisting of all the documents which people in the organisation need to carry out their tasks. These references won't just be for the third level of the organisation, although the majority of them are likely to be.

Strictly speaking, these documents aren't actually part of the quality management manual: in most cases, there would be far too many of them to put together as a single document. However, they are part of the quality management system and are referred to throughout the quality procedures manual itself. Some kind of index to them should be part of the quality management manual, so we have included a guide to workplace references in this book.

## The quality management system and the quality management manual

There is obviously a very close relationship between the quality management system and the quality management manual, and you can't, as they say, have one without the other. There is however the question of which comes first.

In theory, it should be possible to do all the work for the quality management system before you come to write the quality management manual. So all the decision making, resource allocation, formulation of policies and agreement of procedures could happen as part of setting up the quality management system. Writing the quality management manual would then just be a matter of structuring and recording all the decisions about the quality management system that had already been made.

But in practice, the need to create the quality management manual often drives the quality management project (see Figure 3). In effect, the contents list of the quality management manual can act as a plan for implementing the quality management system. This tends to be the approach we assume in this book: when we mention something which should be in the quality management manual, we go on to explain how to go about it.

Although it may seem back to front, it is actually quite a good idea to develop the quality management manual and the quality management system it represents iteratively: that is to say, by making decisions, by recording them in the manual, and by revisiting and revising them as necessary. The discipline of writing things down as they are decided will help to focus decision making, and the structure of the quality management manual will make sure that the quality management system structure is complete.

Quite how you approach the relationship between the quality management manual and the quality management system will depend on how you organise the project as a whole (see Part 4, *Project Management*). But however you do it, make sure they come together in the end.

## Case Study

### *Campion Software – Quality Management is Change Management*

In 1991 the software design and development house Campion completed the successful takeover of a significant rival, Beddowes and Rushton. B&R was in fact capitalised at more than Campion, since it had a hardware products division as well as a software house. The takeover was a bold and well-publicised move, reflecting the expansionism and market confidence of the late 1980s. Overnight Campion more than doubled both its assets and liabilities.

Campion was a well-established and respected company, 15 years old. This represented a long time in this industry. Most of its work was in large business systems software development. Its most recent venture had been into the healthcare market, to develop clinical systems and management databases. Campion had developed a strong management structure and well-defined processes and procedures to ensure that its design and development contracts, which were notoriously difficult to control, were managed effectively. It had benefited in the marketplace from its reputation for reliability at a time when smaller software houses came and went overnight.

Campion was confident not only that it could absorb the financial implications of its takeover of B&R, but also that its management was strong enough to deal with the expansion.

B&R was a subsidiary of the defence contractors Welton & Co. Weltons dated back to the turn of the century and were seen as virtually a government department, so closely were they bound by government standards and regulations for their products. The Ministry of Defence regularly inspected the premises and Weltons took pride in the quality of their work and its conformance to specification. This attitude had been transferred to the newer subsidiary company.

When considering the takeover, Campion had thought carefully about the culture of B&R, its standards and values. Campion was confident that there was a match between the two companies. Both took pride in their reputations for reliability and quality, and had well-developed processes and procedures.

Shortly after the takeover the board of the newly merged company announced that it would apply for BS5750 registration. This would capitalise on the strong management structures that had been developed through the years. The board immediately allocated resources to the project and appointed a project manager from B&R who was familiar with working to government contracts and who had been a chief inspector, and a firm of management consultants to verify the design of the quality management manual. From the start the project went very smoothly. The manual was completed in record time. It was weighty, detailed and complete. It was presented to the management consultants for a 'desktop check', that is a check on its content. The management consultants were able to find very few areas of omission in each of the management processes and procedures the quality manager documented. They were aware of the need to check that these procedures were actually being used and advised on setting up an audit system. Everything seemed to be in order.

The manual was then submitted to the certification body and the Campion board looked forward to registration day. They had ordered the champagne. They had also commissioned a detailed marketing plan showing how registration would become the cornerstone of their next marketing campaign. They would be one of the first in their industry to achieve registration and they believed it would add an important dimension to their reputation. The whole company was aware of the assessors' presence and everyone made sure that their work was carried out particularly efficiently that week.

Late in the evening the news came to the expectant board. Campion had failed to gain registration. The assessors had found that the two parts of the newly merged company were continuing to work as they had always done – differently. This constituted a major example of non-compliance with the manual and the assessors had no option but to fail the company.

The board took some time to try to find out why these problems had not been picked up by the audit process once the quality management system was up and running. They discovered a number of interesting facts:

- the quality manager from B&R was not conversant with the technology being used at the Campion site and didn't really understand their procedures

- as a result, Campion staff had largely signed off their own procedures

- audits had been carried out – but with project managers auditing their own projects. This meant that the differences in how projects were being run had not been picked up.

What the company needed now was a systematic change management programme supporting the merger, which would identify the cultural changes that needed to take place before the two organisations really became one.

The quality system project also had to go back to first principles and look at what was actually happening across the new company, and to build up the processes and procedures from this. The new manual took a year to prepare, but Campion did achieve registration almost exactly two years later than they had anticipated.

# The Quality Policy Manual 4

## The purpose of the quality policy manual

The first part of the quality management manual is the quality policy manual. This is an important document, an introduction to all the other sections of the quality management system, a summary of your quality policy, and how you intend to meet the requirements of ISO9000. Anyone reading through your quality policy manual should come away with considerable insight into the primary functions of your organisation and how these functions are managed and controlled.

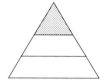

**Figure 4** *The quality policy manual relates to the top level of the organisation*

The quality policy manual serves as a kind of public noticeboard where your organisation can pin up its policies and communicate through them to people inside the organisation and beyond. These policy statements must come from the top of the organisation, to signal clearly just how important senior management believes quality management to be (Figure 4).

## Audiences for the quality policy manual

People both inside and outside the organisation have an interest in the quality policy manual. There are at least four different audiences which you need to address, one internal and three external.

### The internal audience

The internal audience for the quality policy manual is made up of the organisation's managers and, ultimately, all its staff. The manual will act as a reference guide to organisational policy, a reminder of the management standards which have to be met in sales, resource planning, purchasing, production, training, invoicing, administration and all other functions. The quality policy manual is the touchstone for measuring success in quality management.

### *External audience 1: Assessors of quality management systems*

External assessors will make their preliminary judgement about your readiness for registration from the quality management manual. The assessors know all they need to know about the requirements of quality management standards. What they need to learn from your quality policy manual is how your particular organisation has interpreted these requirements. This is particularly important if your business does not conform to a straightforward production model. For example, the quality management assessor needs to know how your organisation controls product or service quality, and how examples of non-conformance are identified and recorded. You will be able to show this easily enough if your organisation's products can be measured and counted. But in service businesses like consultancy or health, products are largely invisible. The quality policy manual has to show the assessor how your organisation has adapted the principles of assessment and control, in these different settings.

### *External audience 2: Clients and customers*

Your more important, or more curious, clients or customers will be interested in reading your quality policy manual, particularly your quality policy statement. It will help your clients and customers to understand the level of service they can expect from you, as you set off on a process of quality improvement. It will also help to explain any new procedures you may be adopting.

There is a genuine curiosity among clients and customers to see whether the letters and numbers of quality management registration make any difference to the service they receive. They can expect too much: you will not become perfect overnight. Stories abound about companies who get their registration certificates and let down their biggest customers the next day. It is much better to let your clients or customers read your policy manual and understand what you are really trying to do, than to allow them to build up false expectations about what registration will mean for them.

### *External audience 3: Suppliers*

Quality management includes the selection and management of suppliers. This is part of the process of building strategic supplier alliances. You will have to introduce procedures for vetting and monitoring your suppliers, which may well have an impact on aspects of your suppliers' businesses. If your organisation is large enough, it may even require suppliers to register for a quality management standard themselves. Your suppliers will therefore have a direct interest in the quality policy manual as it will affect their businesses.

## The style of the quality policy manual

For general guidance on writing clearly and effectively, see Chapter 7, *Writing the Quality Management Manual*. Because the quality policy manual addresses four different audiences, finding the right style is going to be quite difficult. An analysis of the four audiences, indeed, shows that there are few shared areas of knowledge and expertise (see Figure 5).

Knowledge of the organisation

|  | | High | Low |
|---|---|---|---|
| Technical knowledge of quality management systems | High | The quality manager | Assessors |
| | Low | Managers | Clients |

**Figure 5** *The four audiences of the quality policy manual*

Managers are experts in how their organisation works, but not necessarily in quality management. Assessors are experts in ISO9000, but know little about any particular organisation. Clients and customers are usually experts in neither, but want to understand the quality policy manual.

You will not be able to avoid making specialist references of one sort or another as you write the quality policy manual. Indeed, quality management assessors will expect to see management activities described in the vocabulary of the quality standard. You will need to find a skilful balance between a style which accommodates your more general readers, and a style which relates to the particular and specialist knowledge of the other audiences. Consider including explanations with any specialist vocabulary or concepts you use, if you are not sure that what you have written will be understood by the people who need to understand it.

# The content of the quality policy manual

The quality policy manual can be divided into six sections:

1. Introduction

2. Policy statements

3. Organisational structure

4. Management responsibility and authority

5. Management review

6. The quality management system and its relationship to ISO9000 requirements.

## Introduction

It is useful to have an introductory section. In it you can put your organisation's quality programme in context by introducing the organisation and its quality management system.

A typical introductory section to the quality policy manual would cover things like:

- what quality management standard you are using

- how the quality management manual is organised and controlled

- who the people are in the organisation who are most closely identified with implementing it.

## Policy statements

### The mission statement

You may already have a mission statement which expresses your company's objectives and acts as a focus for the core business. If you have a mission statement, you can include it in the quality policy manual – an item on the noticeboard which helps to explain what your organisation is all about.

If you don't have a mission statement, it is worth considering why not. If the honest answer is because you don't know what your mission is, you won't get far with implementing a quality management system. Your organisation must have a mission, or at least a clear, commonly held understanding of its purpose, if the quality management system is going to work.

In the early days of ISO9000, companies such as the large utilities or defence-based industries didn't need to ask such questions. But now it is interesting to note how the question of why the organisation exists has become more and more relevant to quality management systems, particularly as ISO9000 is applied to the non-manufacturing industry sectors of account-ancy, law, surveying, the health service, education or government.

Adopting the ISO9000 way of management won't tell you what your mission is, but you are not likely to succeed with it unless you know.

### The quality policy statement

For the quality policy manual, you must have a quality policy statement (see section 4.1.1 of ISO9001). This is a statement of your policy specifically about customers and about quality issues. There may be some overlap between the mission statement and the quality policy statement. But the quality policy statement is entirely about customers and how your product or service will meet their requirements.

If your organisation is very large with significant management responsibility devolved to division and departments, these divisions or departments can take responsibility for defining their own quality objectives in relation to the company's overall quality policy.

### Signing the quality policy statement

Seeing through the implementation of the quality policy state-ment will be quite a demanding exercise for senior management. It is now common policy for the chief executive of the organisa-tion to sign the quality policy statement. This lets everyone see clearly that the drive for quality management has the under-standing and support of the highest level of the organisation.

# Policy, mission, vision and value statements

Here is a selection of policy, mission and value statements. Notice how these statements are about what the organisation wants to achieve for itself and its shareholders, as well as for its customers.

It is often quite difficult to distinguish between the various kinds of policy statements, but in the end it doesn't matter what you call it, as long as it expresses succinctly something that rings true to your organisation. Too many statements ring hollow.

### Polycell mission statement

Polycell aspires to be the best Brand in its trading sector and provide the highest return on sales and investment for its parent Williams Holdings.

By implication our customers are always foremost in our mind whether it be for innovation, quality or service. We never assume our markets will remain stable so through the highest standards of communication and training our employees are encouraged to extend the boundaries of excellence in everything they do.

Due to the speed we move, good judgement, honesty and integrity are benchmarks for a culture and Brand that is obsessed with success and continuous improvement.

### Marks and Spencer value statement

Selling clothing for the family, fashion for the home, and a range of fine foods – all representing high standards of quality and value.

Creating an attractive, efficient shopping environment for customers.

Providing a friendly, helpful service from well-trained staff.

Sharing mutually beneficial, long-term partnerships with suppliers, encouraging them to use modern and efficient production techniques.

Supporting British industry and buying abroad only when new ideas, technology, quality and value are not available in the UK.

Ensuring staff and shareholders share in the success of the company.

Constantly seeking to improve quality standards in all areas of the company's operations.

Fostering good human relations with customers, staff, suppliers and community.

### British Airways mission statement

We have a clear ambition. We want British Airways to be the best and most successful airline in the world because we believe it will be good for our passengers, it will be good for our shareholders, it will be good for the people who work for us and it will be good for the people of Britain. What's wrong with that?

# Quality policy statements

Here are a selection of quality policy statements.

## Brightwells

We will provide air-driven fluid pumps and hydraulic power packs that fully meet our customers' requirements and give reliability in service. Thus it is our intention to satisfy customers' needs first time, on time and every time at good value to them and profitability to the company. All our employees will strive to support this goal. This policy is implemented through our Quality System which operates in accordance with BS5750 and the international standard ISO9000.

Signature........................................................................MD

## The Xerox quality policy

Xerox is a quality company. Quality is the basic business principle for Xerox. Quality means providing our external and internal customers with innovative products and services that fully satisfy their requirements. Quality improvement is the job of every Xerox employee.

## Johnson Matthey

We set and strive to achieve standards of quality which ensure defect-free operations and administration. We do it right the first time to the satisfaction of customers, shareholders and ourselves.

*Objectives*
Quality first. All employees put Johnson Matthey quality first in their approach to their task. Education. We educate ourselves so that we fully understand the requirements of our jobs.
*Products and Processes*
We design our products and processes to achieve defect-free operation.
*Organisation and measurement*
We organise and measure our activities to meet requirements first time.
*Cost of quality*
We invest in Quality and continually reduce the costs of non-quality performance.
*Suppliers*
We require defect-free materials and services from our suppliers and help to improve their quality processes.
*Teamwork*
We maintain the culture and climate in which efficiency, innovation and quality performance are encouraged and fostered.

# Organisational structure

▲ If you don't have a clear management structure, you should refer to a textbook on organisational theory for guidance on how to develop an appropriate structure for your business. Some examples are:
Peter Drucker, *The Practice of Management* (Butterworth-Heinemann, 1992)
Charles Handy, *Understanding Organisations* (Penguin, 1992)
Wilfred Brown, *Organisation*, (Heinemann Educational, 1971)
D S Pugh (Ed), *Organisation Theory* (Penguin, 1990)
Henry L Sisk, *Management and Organisations* (South Western Publishing Company, 1989)

In this section of the quality policy manual you must start to build up a picture of how your organisation works, so that your external audiences in particular can gain a more detailed understanding of who you are and what you are trying to achieve. You can include here any information which helps to do this: for example, some companies like to show site layouts and locations, to make descriptions of processes and procedures easier to understand.

Most of your attention, however, should be given to describing your organisational structure. The best way to start is to look for an organisation chart. If you're lucky, you'll only have to ask your personnel department for a copy. Otherwise you will have to draw up such a chart to reflect the structure that you have, or if you work in a small, relatively informal organisation, you may even have to start from scratch and work out what your management structure actually is, before you can formalise it for the quality policy manual.

Interestingly, though, you will probably find that your organisation chart will change as a result of the quality management system. This is because you will be analysing your business processes and thinking about how best to control your business.

## Types of organisational structure

There are many types of organisational structure, but they can broadly be divided into two kinds:

- *line management structures.* Authority passes down from the top of the organisation, through a chain or line of managers, to the workforce at the bottom. Potentially, line management structures make questions of control and responsibility very clear.

▲ Project-based structures are also known as matrix structures

- *project-based structures.* The roles and responsibilities in the organisation are only partly fixed. Functional roles in a hierarchical sense do exist to a certain extent, but staff are not bound by them. Individual roles and responsibilities are also defined according to the project that needs to be undertaken. This structure is good for managing a work pattern which consists of separate projects, all of them needing a different mix of skills. It is very flexible and makes the most of the skills and expertise in the organisation.

You may recognise characteristics of both structures in your organisation, but there will be a dominant style which will determine what your organisational chart will look like.

## Organisation charts

When you are clear about what kind of organisational structure you have, you should prepare an organisation chart for the quality policy manual (see sections 4.1.2.1 and 4.1.2.2 of ISO9001). Organisation charts need to show:

- how the lines of authority through the company are organised – around product lines (eg refrigerator division, washing machine division), or around functions (sales department, production department)

- how many levels of authority there are, and the titles of the roles in the hierarchy

- what formalised direct and cross-reporting relationships exist between lines of management responsibility.

As well as showing management roles, you must also show roles which are important for your quality management system:

- the quality management representative (this role includes auditing)

- the deputy management representative

- the role responsible for carrying out management reviews

- any other key quality management roles, such as quality controller, inspector and so on.

Don't use names on the chart, because the people may change – use job titles.

## Preparing organisation charts for line management structures

Line management structures are easy to chart because they consist of fixed, direct relationships.

Represent roles by rectangular boxes; show direct lines of authority by straight lines between boxes. If there are important cross-reporting relationships, you can show these with a dotted line.

The diagram will be in the shape of a pyramid. At the top is the chief executive. Then comes the second layer of management, which reports directly to the head of the organisation, then the next layer and so on. It is not usually necessary to include the workforce in the chart: you only need to include posts of managerial or supervisory responsibility.

Figure 6 shows the line management structure in a small manufacturing company. Notice how key quality management roles have been included.

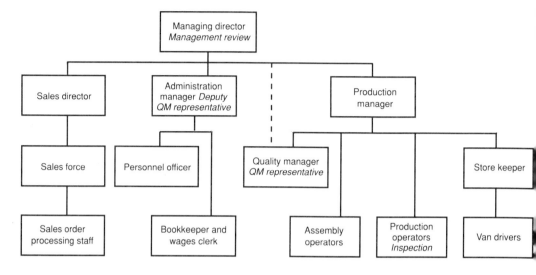

**Figure 6** *Organisation chart for a line management company*

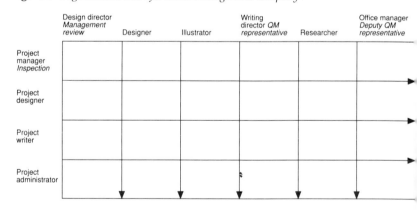

**Figure 7** *Organisation chart for a project-based structure (1)*

## Preparing organisation charts for project-based structures

Because these structures are so flexible, they are not so easy to represent diagrammatically. One way is to use a matrix. The horizontal axis represents the functions of the organisation, the fixed roles. The vertical axis represents the task-related or potentially variable roles. The matrix shows how the functional roles and task-related roles potentially combine.

In the example in Figure 7 the company specialises in multi-skilled writing and design projects. Functional roles are listed along the top of the matrix. For each piece of work, people with the appropriate skills are selected and given one of the project roles.

Another way of showing a matrix structure is to start with line management relationships, and then to use dotted lines to show how people take on different roles for different projects (see Figure 8).

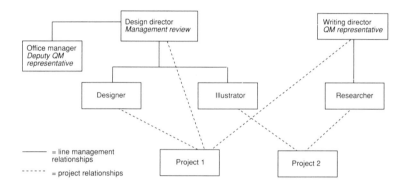

**Figure 8**  *Organisation chart for a project-based structure (2)*

## Management responsibility and authority

Your organisation chart will have identified key roles, and shown the relationships between them. You should now work through these roles in more detail, writing down a brief description of responsibilities and reporting relationships.

Line management roles are easy to describe in terms of responsibility and authority. For example, if the production company on page 54 has a problem with the quality of one of its products, there is a clear line of responsibility up from the assembly operators, who inspect the finished products, to the production quality manager and the administration manager, who manage the quality system and who will be responsible for corrective action and any necessary changes in procedures.

Roles in project management structures are more difficult to pin down. For example, in the writing and design company on

◆ Role description: managing director. The managing director is responsible for:
– the overall management of the company
– the overall strategy and future direction of the company with particular attention to the company's
  – products and services
  – systems
  – employees
  – customers
  – suppliers
– marketing and advertising activities in order to promote existing and new products and processes.

page 55 everyone has a specialist role based on their skills. These specialist roles are hierarchical: there is a design director role and a junior designer role, for example. But there are also roles which change within each project, such as the project manager, or the project designer or the project researcher. A junior designer can in fact be the project designer, working to the project manager rather than to the design director.

Obviously you can't show exactly how each of your projects will be structured on an organisational chart. At this level, you can only show potential relationships.

What you must do therefore is to define responsibilities separately for each project. This is referred to in the quality management standard as the *Quality Plan* (see ISO9004 Guidelines).

## Management review

You should state here your intention to carry out management review. Management review is the process by which senior management regularly evaluates all aspects of the quality management system. The concept of management review is very important if you are to make sure that your system develops over time and does not become a fossilised and irrelevant piece of bureaucracy (see section 4.1.3 of ISO9001).

In setting out your management review process, you should state:

- who will lead the review

- how often it will be held

- what information sources will be used by the review (eg quality records, audits)

- what the management review objectives are

- how the review findings will be presented (eg in a report, at a board meeting).

Management review looks at all the information which the quality management system has been collecting, to make sure this information doesn't get lost but rather feeds back into the organisation at the highest level where appropriate changes can be made in response to any problems which have emerged.

# The quality management system and its conformance with ISO9000 requirements

In the final section of the quality policy manual, you should provide an overview of the quality management system in your organisation. You should define here:

- the scope of your quality management system for registration

- the relationship between your quality management system and ISO9000 requirements.

## *The scope of your quality management system*

Whenever a quality management system is mentioned, the assumption tends to be that the system covers all the products and processes in the organisation, like a large umbrella. But this need not always be so. On the contrary, it may make very good sense for your organisation to limit the scope of its quality management system, at least in the first instance (see Figure 9).

One limitation, of course, will be imposed by the kind of business you are. ISO9001/BS5750 Part 1 covers product supply and design; ISO9002/BS5750 Part 2 covers production and installation. You need to be clear about the scope of your business and what part of the standard applies to you.

Another case for limiting the application of the standard might occur if you have a number of different products or services. Rather than trying to create a very large umbrella system all at once, you may decide to:

The whole-company approach

- define different quality management systems for each group of products or services – a number of smaller, different umbrellas

Different approaches for different products or services

- develop the quality management system for one group first and roll out the quality programme through the rest of the organisation later on. For example, you might wish to register head office and one major regional office to start with and add in other regional offices as they are ready

**Figure 9** *Defining the scope of the quality management standard*

- develop the quality management system for key products or services only.

If you are taking any of these options, define the scope of your quality management system in this part of the quality policy manual. Assessors are generally sympathetic to such partial registrations, as long as they do not go against the spirit of the standard or seem irrelevant to the core business.

### Statement of conformance with ISO9000 requirements

To complete the quality policy manual, you must show how your quality management system conforms with the requirements of ISO9000. You can do this by listing the elements of the quality management standard and cross-referencing them to particular procedures you have in place, to show how the requirements of the quality management standard are met by your organisation.

Procedures are of course in the next part of the quality management manual, the quality procedures manual. This means that you can't complete the conformance section until both parts of the manual have been prepared. In fact this may well be the very last section you do. You can use it as a check that all the standards have been covered.

The quality management assessor will find the statement of conformance to ISO9000 requirements both useful and necessary. It shows the assessor that there are no gaps in the content of your manual and gives evidence of exactly how quality management requirements are fulfilled. Information about particular requirements which is threaded through the procedures can be brought together to give a complete overview of your quality management system.

### How to set out the statement of conformance with ISO9000

There are a number of ways of setting out the statement of conformance. The method you choose will depend on:

- how you structure the procedures

- how much comment you want to make about how you have interpreted the management standard requirements.

### Using charts

You can use a matrix chart to show where the ISO9000 requirements and your procedures relate. List your organisation's procedures down the side of the chart and the categories of the ISO9000 management standard along the top (see Figure 10). Then mark the points where the procedures relate to the management standard requirements.

You should think about using a chart like this if the procedures showing conformance with the standard tend to be in a number of different places in your manual. The chart provides an effective visual overview of the whole quality management system and focuses scattered elements. It will help you to find particular procedures as well as matching them to the standard.

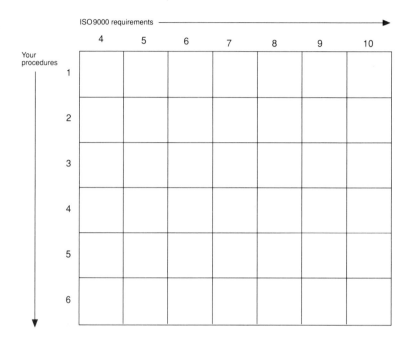

**Figure 10** *Chart showing conformance with ISO9000 requirements*

## *Using lists*

Another way to approach the task is to list the ISO9000 requirements and write out the procedures which relate to each requirement beside it (see Figure 11). This method will take more time to put together than the chart, but the result is a very clear and easy-to-follow statement of conformance. The method won't work so well with scattered references: use it where there are straightforward areas of correspondence between the standard and the procedures.

| ISO9000 requirements | Procedures |
|---|---|
| Write here the number and title of each quality management requirement. | Write here the number and title of each procedure which fulfils the requirement. |

**Figure 11** *Comparing ISO9000 requirements with procedures*


## Using separate sections

As well as using charts or lists, you could take each of the ISO9000 requirements separately and then describe how they are covered by your quality management system. The description must include cross-references to the quality procedures manual. This approach is the most labour-intensive and does not give such an instant overview of the quality management system as the other two methods, but it does give you the space to explain in as much detail as you need how you have interpreted and covered each requirement (see Figure 12).

| ISO9000 requirement |
|---|
| Write here a description of how you are carrying out this requirement. |
| Include cross-references to the procedures which relate to this requirement. |

**Figure 12** *Describing in detail how procedures conform to ISO9000 requirements*

When you have completed the quality policy manual, you will have given each of its audiences an overview of both your organisation and your quality management system. The information given in the quality policy manual is summarised in Figure 13. You are ready to move to the quality management procedures, the next level of detail which shows how the quality management system actually works.

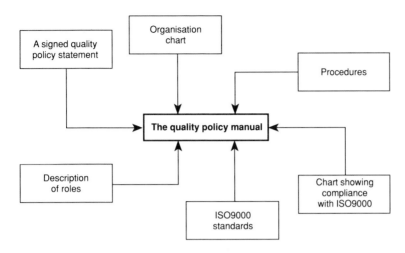

**Figure 13** *A summary of information for the quality policy manual*

## Case Study

### *The Andrews and Dale Partnership – Bringing Policy Issues into the Open*

Alan Rogers settled himself at his desk and looked at the folder in front of him with satisfaction. Alan had been working as a quality management consultant at DPS Consulting for nearly a year and this was his first assignment as project manager. In the folder on his desk were all the notes his team had made over the past two weeks about the Andrews and Dale Partnership, a successful architect's practice. Andrews and Dale was interested in being one of the first in their industry to register for BS5750. The founding partner, John Andrews, had given Alan his reasons.

'Being successful in this field is as much about good management as talent,' he had said. 'We run a tight ship here at the Andrews and Dale Partnership and I don't think it will be difficult for us to get through registration first time round. We want our customers to know that we're professional and that we won't let them down.'

In the two weeks that followed, everything Alan saw, and everything Alan's team reported, made him more and more inclined to agree with John Andrews' assessment. Everywhere they looked, the team saw evidence of neatly kept records and well-organised files.

There were six partners in the firm and three administrative staff. Everyone had been keen to find time to talk to the consultancy team and to give detailed accounts of how projects were managed, from initial contact with the client to the final deliverables. In Alan's file were records of all these interviews and copies of well-presented procedures and management documentation. All he had to do now was to familiarise himself with the material and put together his recommendations.

Alan sipped his cup of coffee and set to work. As he worked, he made notes about where the items of information which had been collected belonged in the quality management system. Gradually the pile of papers from the Andrews and Dale Partnership grew smaller, as Alan allocated the content of the papers to the QMS categories.

Alan felt very pleased with his day's work. He remembered how anxious he had been about the assignment when he first learned that he would be in charge of it. This was the first project of which he had full charge and he was aware that a creative, service-based organisation might be rather difficult to define. He had also expected that DPS would meet opposition from the architects themselves, since their working practices would be under scrutiny. But he had no need to worry. The company knew where it was going and was anxious to help the DPS team.

Next day Alan opened up the Andrews and Dale folder confidently and re-read his work of the day before. It was then that he realised for the first time that he had a problem. His analysis certainly showed that all aspects of the QMS were being addressed, as his team had reported. But it also showed that everyone in the company was doing things in a different way. Some of these differences were small, such as how each partner liked to set out an invoice. Variations like these were very common in companies who had not had to go through the discipline of registration before. One of the reasons why DPS had been called in was to pick up these differences and to recommend which practice should be adopted.

Other differences, however, were about policy. For example, some partners worked closely with their clients from the start of the project and believed that it was important to listen to the client and to compromise on a design, even if that meant making the design less innovative or introducing elements that the architect personally did not like.

Penelope Brotherston typified this approach She had joined the Partnership quite recently and said she enjoyed the challenge of creating solutions which were what the client really wanted.

'People often don't know what they want,' she had said. 'My job is to listen to their ideas and try to understand who they are and what they need. A quality service is one which gives people what they want, at the price they can afford.'

Other partners had a different approach to clients. John Andrews explained:

'As you get more experienced, you get better at dealing with clients. If you aren't careful, they end up using all your time in meetings and phone calls when you should be getting on with the work. They would be pretty annoyed if you charged them by the minute for the time they use, but from my point of view, that's what I have to worry about, how my time is paid for. And if you allow them to get too involved with what you are doing, they will spoil the integrity of your design. After all, they are not the experts, whatever they may like to think. I'm the one they should listen to.'

Another difference which emerged centred around what the partners saw their company as representing. This conflict was present between the founding partners themselves.

John Andrews wanted the company to be seen as professional and businesslike. This fitted in with his ideas about clients. Clients should be clear about the service they were getting and leave the architect to get on with the job.

The other founder of the Partnership, Brian Dale, agreed that this was important. However, his vision of the company was quite different.

'Anyone can be businesslike,' he said. 'Of course we want to be good managers, and to make profits. But that isn't why people will come to us. They won't say, well, we don't like their buildings, but they keep good records and come in on budget. We must put our effort into constantly evaluating what we do and get a reputation for really good work, so that we can keep attracting new partners with talent.'

As Alan read through all the comments he had collected under the quality policy heading, he realised he had a big problem. As things were, he could not honestly say that the company had a coherent quality policy at all. Any issues he raised about the company's vision of itself and its understanding of quality would be sure to start divisive arguments. And in theory, this would mean that they could not go for BS5750 certification, as they wanted.

On the other hand, the Partnership was a successful company which encouraged sound management practices. Surely this was what the BS5750 standard was all about? Would it not be better to ignore the question of policy and let the company go ahead, with different ideas existing happily side by side?

Early the next day, Alan called an emergency meeting of the partners and bluntly stated the problem he had uncovered. In fact none of the partners was very surprised. All agreed that this was a good opportunity to talk openly about some of their differences to see if they could reach agreement. The partners arranged for an away-day and six weeks later were able to report to Alan that they had reached a consensus on what quality really meant in their practice. The atmosphere between the partners seemed to be much more relaxed. Penelope Brotherston confided to Alan that she had been quite unhappy before the away-day, feeling isolated and out of sympathy with the others. 'I feel we're actually all pulling in the same direction now,' she explained. 'Facing this issue has made a very positive difference to this practice.'

# The Quality Procedures Manual 5

## The purpose of the quality procedures manual

The first part of the quality management manual, the quality policy manual, is primarily about strategy. It defines the organisation's quality management system in terms of its policies, objectives and structure.

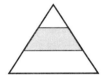

The second part of the manual, the quality procedures manual, moves to the tactical level (see Figure 14). It is above all about practice, the operational detail of the quality management system. In it you need to define and describe:

**Figure 14** *The quality procedures manual relates to the middle level of the organisation*

- the management processes in the organisation

- the procedures which must be followed to make those processes work smoothly and uniformly.

This part of the quality manual is the operational core of the whole quality management system. It sets up a detailed model of how your organisation should operate, against which quality management assessors will evaluate your actual practices for registration.

## The audience for the quality procedures manual

As with the quality policy manual, there are both internal and external audiences for the quality procedures manual. However, since the quality procedures manual is mainly about internal procedures (although some will concern clients and suppliers), its primary audience is also mainly internal.

### The internal audience

The primary internal audience for the quality procedures manual is middle management, the people who work at the second level of the organisation. These are the people who are responsible for developing the procedures and for making sure they are followed.

Of course, anyone at any level of the organisation will be able to consult the quality procedures manual out of interest or to check out particular points of procedure. But this part of the manual will have a special relevance for those who helped to develop it, who work to it every day and who have to ensure that others do so.

### The external audience

There is an external audience for the quality procedures manual – your external assessors will be concerned with its content. They will want to check that all the relevant management processes are represented and that your procedures cover them adequately. In fact, when you have finished writing the quality management manual they will carry out a desktop check or audit for you, so that you do not find yourself wasting time implementing procedures which are inadequate or incomplete (see Chapter 11, *Assessment and After*).

The assessors will be in a good position to judge whether the people who use the manual find it effective. Otherwise you can have a free hand with the layout and presentation of the quality management manual – the assessors won't comment on how you achieve this.

## The style of the quality procedures manual

The style of the quality procedures manual must, above all, be appropriate for the middle managers who are going to use it most. Because the middle managers in an organisation will seem to form an identifiable and coherent group of people, who are either familiar with the organisation's procedural issues or who, as newcomers, are about to become so, you will tend to assume that you are addressing an informed and motivated audience. You won't feel that you have to explain things in the kind of detail that would be necessary for an uninformed or external audience, for example.

However, remember that your audience will be working under pressure. You must make sure that the procedures you prepare really are easy to use – that is, quick to find and immediately clear in meaning. If they aren't, your audience will quickly become frustrated and give in to the pressure of work by doing things their own way, the way, very probably, they have been doing things for years.

You could say, therefore, that the success or failure of the implementation of the whole quality management system is linked to how well you present the procedures. It is worth spending the time to find a style which communicates effectively with the people in your organisation. For more guidance on presenting and writing the quality manual, see Chapter 7, *Writing the Quality Management Manual*, and Chapter 8, *Designing the Quality Management Manual*.

## The content of the quality procedures manual

The quality procedures manual consists of:

* management processes
* quality management procedures.

It's easy enough to say this, but in practice writing down this information is a major undertaking. This is true for all sizes of organisation: even if you belong to a small company, you should not expect it to be particularly straightforward, or to be done overnight.

And even when you have identified and documented all your processes and procedures, you then have the task of putting together the quality procedures manual and of relating the procedures to ISO9000 requirements.

There are no rules in the quality management standard about how to put together the quality procedures manual. In fact, there are probably as many ways of doing it as there are manuals. Our suggestions in this chapter are based on years of experience with a wide variety of organisations. Hopefully you will find them useful in helping you to deal confidently with the content of your own quality procedures manual. Figure 15 shows the relationship of processes and procedures to the quality manual.

You will find a worked example of a section of a quality procedures manual in the Appendix (see page 193).

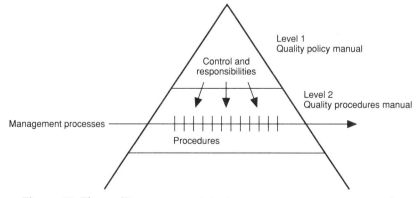

**Figure 15** *The quality management system – management processes and procedures*

## Management processes

As you begin to look at what goes on in your organisation, you will be able to identify groups of management activities sharing a common theme or purpose. These are management processes. Start the quality procedures manual by establishing what your organisation's key management processes are. If you don't think about these processes before starting to write down your procedures, you will very quickly get lost in a wealth of detail and lose sight of the shape of your organisation as a whole.

◆ Examples of management processes which all organisations tend to have are:
– sales and marketing
– accounts and finance
– quality assurance.
Management processes which can vary widely from organisation to organisation are:
– operations management
– infrastructure management
– project management.

As regards content, there are some management processes which are more or less common to all businesses. Others vary considerably between organisations, depending on what exactly the company does: whether it sells services or products, or whether it makes, assembles or simply stocks products, or whether it sells services and products, and so on.

A useful way to think about your management processes is as functions with the kinds of titles which would be given to departments in large organisations. For example, you would expect any large organisation to have departments in:

• sales and marketing

• finance

• purchasing

• production

• distribution

• personnel.

These are management processes. To start the process of identifying your own, try asking yourself questions like:

• who exactly are our customers?

• what are our products or services?

• what functions do we have?

Below are examples of some of the things which drive management processes. You will probably discover more, as you think about how your organisation works and why it works as it does.

### Time-line management processes

The concept of the time-line governs all the key strategic management processes in your organisation. The time-line starts with an order from a customer or client and finishes when the order has been fulfilled and the goods or services paid for.

As the order progresses through the organisation, different activities take place which are essential to getting it through: essential to your existence and survival (see Figure 16). Time-line management processes are very important and are a good place for you to start identifying your particular processes.

**Figure 16** *The time-line*

## Time-independent management processes

Of course, there are some management processes which are not time-dependent. They are made up of longer-term, ongoing activities which support the time-dependent processes, but which are not tied to them in time.

◆ Examples of time-independent processes:
– marketing
– quality assurance
– recruitment
– research and development.

## Customer-driven management processes

Another way of identifying different management processes is to look at your range of customers. This can be a very revealing thing to do, since it is actually quite likely that different customers will want you to do things in different ways. An extreme example of this is the company which called in a team of quality management consultants to sort out the many divergent procedures which they had accumulated, sometimes up to five different ways of carrying out virtually the same task.

The team of consultants found that actually this degree of divergence was necessary. Their processes were driven by the diversity of their customer base. Customers were in different countries and it was necessary to service them using different procedures. The company had tried to look at its management processes as functions, instead of customer-driven time-lines. The quality management consultancy team was able quite simply to restructure procedures by client and in doing so cleared up years of confusion (see Figure 17).

## Management processes and ISO9000

You won't find management processes outlined in ISO9000. As with so many features of the standard, the reason for this is probably historical: large manufacturing companies would have had more or less the same management processes, so this analysis framework wasn't necessary.

The standard of course provides a list of all the management activities that need to be documented in the quality procedures

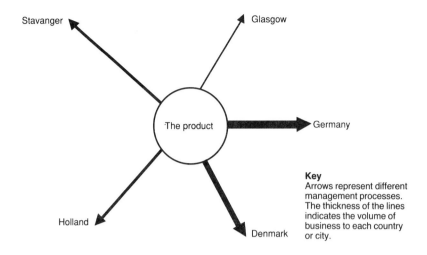

**Figure 17** *Customer-driven management processes*

manual. But don't be tempted to start at the beginning and apply the list indiscriminately to your organisation. Not everything that is mentioned in the standard will necessarily be relevant to your organisation. And if you are a service business, many parts of the standard will clearly not be relevant. Your procedures must be firmly rooted in the management processes which really do need to happen in your organisation.

A good example of how you may have to adapt and interpret the manufacturing-based standard ISO9000 is given by the experiences of two hospital radiography departments. These departments had to start interpreting the standard by defining who their customers really were.

The first department defined the consultant as the customer and the X-ray patients as 'purchaser supplied material'. It looked at time-lines from the perspective of the consultants, so that the process control requirement centred on the doctors.

The second department made the fundamentally different decision to define the patient as the customer and the consultant as a resource. This department looked at the time-line from the point of view of the patients and set out to document, control and improve everything that happened to them.

This difference in applying the standard not surprisingly resulted in some markedly different practices. However, both are

legitimate as far as the quality management standard is concerned – even if we have all been to the first department and
profoundly wish we'd gone to the second one instead.

## Models for management processes

To help you see how the quality management standard relates to
management processes, you can divide the ISO9000 quality
management requirements into four categories (see Figure 18):

- business management
- operations management
- quality assurance
- quality control.

Notice that we put the inspection and test requirement in both
operations management and quality control. In operations management, inspection is carried out by the person who is doing the
job. In quality control, an independent person carries out a
quality control check.

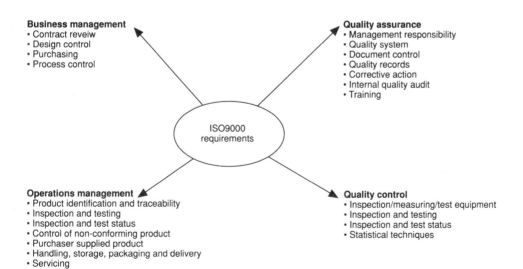

**Business management**
- Contract reveiw
- Design control
- Purchasing
- Process control

**Quality assurance**
- Management responsibility
- Quality system
- Document control
- Quality records
- Corrective action
- Internal quality audit
- Training

ISO9000 requirements

**Operations management**
- Product identification and traceability
- Inspection and testing
- Inspection and test status
- Control of non-conforming product
- Purchaser supplied product
- Handling, storage, packaging and delivery
- Servicing

**Quality control**
- Inspection/measuring/test equipment
- Inspection and testing
- Inspection and test status
- Statistical techniques

**Figure 18** *The management processes model*

*The content of the quality management manual*

### Adapting the management processes model

▲ You should explain any differences between your processes and the standard in the quality policy manual.

The four categories of management processes derived from the ISO9000 standard will form a useful point of comparison with the management processes you have identified for yourself. It will help you to see where your business corresponds with the standard and where there are areas of difference.

- *Business management* All businesses have elements of business management, whether they are production-based or service-based.

- *Operations management* Operations management will be different in a production company and in a service business.

- *Quality control* The quality control category defines processes for independent inspection. These might be checking goods-out in a production company, or the partners' review in an accountancy or legal practice.

- *Quality assurance* Quality assurance requirements apply to all companies seeking ISO9000 registration. Here you must focus on improving all the other elements of the quality management system, using tools for problem solving and for adding value to the registration process.

It is worth repeating here that you must not try to impose a false shape on your organisation just so that it fits the standard. Remember the experience of Cinderella's ugly sisters. The shoe didn't fit no matter how hard they tried. Your quality management system won't work if you do this, and the ISO9000 assessors will pick that up straight away. The requirements of the standard may remind you of some gaps that you have in your system: you shouldn't leave parts of it out without due care and consideration. But if you don't do some of the activities, say so, and also include all that you do.

Figures 19 to 22 are some models of typical management processes you would expect to find in different kinds of organisations. These models show the kinds of variations that occur and may help you to identify the model which is right for you.

# Business A

**Business management** ⟶ • Marketing
- Sales activities
- Order processing/contracts
- Purchasing of materials and professional services
- Resource planning
- Scheduling
- Project review
- Project delivery
- Project completion
- Accounts and invoicing

**Operations management** ⟶ • Recruitment
- Training
- Computer systems
- Administration

**Quality assurance** ⟶ • Quality records
- Corrective action
- Audit
- Management review
- Document control
- Management responsibility
- Quality system

**Quality control (as necessary)** ⟶ • Assignment/peer reviews
- Customer service
- Project sign-off

**Figure 19** *Management processes in a professional service business*

# Business B

**Business management** ⟶ • Sales enquiries/quotations
 • Sales orders
 • Technical queries
 • Sourcing policy
 • Supplier assessment
 • Purchasing
 • Stock review
 • Invoicing

**Operations management** ⟶ • Goods in
 • Stores
 • Stock control
 • Order picking
 • Packaging/despatch
 • Transport
 • Returns

**Quality assurance** ⟶ • Quality records
 • Corrective action
 • Audit
 • Management review
 • Document control
 • Training
 • Management responsibility
 • Quality system

**Quality control (as necessary)** ⟶ • Calibration
 • Inspection and testing
 • Sampling plans
 • Certificates of conformity/traceability

**Figure 20** *Management processes in a stockist company*

# Business C

**Business management** ➤
- Pre-tender
- Quotation
- Order processing/contracts
- Setup/quality plan
- Resourcing/scheduling
- Project control
- Purchasing
- Project review
- Invoicing

**Operations management** ➤
- Site control
- Site stores
- Variation/completion
- Technical library

**Quality assurance** ➤
- Quality records
- Corrective action
- Audit
- Management review
- Document control
- Training
- Management responsibility
- Quality system

**Quality control (as necessary)** ➤
- Surveying
- Testing
- Completion certificate

**Figure 21** *Management processes in a contracting company*

# Business D

**Business management** ⟶ • Development/engineering
• Sales enquiry
• Sales order processing
• Production planning
• Production control
• Stock control
• Purchasing
• Production processes
• Invoicing

**Operations management** ⟶ • Production
• Goods in
• Stores
• Goods out
• Assembly
• Test
• Packaging/transport/delivery

**Quality assurance** ⟶ • Quality records
• Corrective action
• Audit
• Management review
• Document control
• Training
• Management responsibility
• Quality system

**Quality control (as necessary)** ⟶ • Receiving inspection
• In-process inspection
• Final inspection
• Calibration
• Statistical techniques

**Figure 22** *Management processes in a manufacturing company*

## *Presenting management processes*

Identifying your management processes will give you a good picture of what is happening in your organisation, and of how it all fits together. It is important to communicate this to the users of the quality procedures manual.

Not all quality procedures manuals provide such an overview. Indeed, one school of thought says that people should only be burdened with what they need to know. But in fact one company, by taking this policy to its logical conclusion, actually proved the opposite. This company gave sections of the quality procedures manual to departments, so that everyone only had what was relevant to them. This sounds logical and economical, but it was in fact a very unpopular move. Staff wanted to see how the whole organisation worked, what other departments did and how their department fitted into the bigger picture.

It is also the case that people will not understand the significance of what you are asking them to do unless they can see interdependence between their work and that of others in the organisation. Having an overview will help them to do this.

So present management processes clearly. You can:

- list them
- depict them in a diagram.

### *Listing management processes*

You can simply list out your management processes and the activities you are including in each one. Give this list plenty of space. It should take up the whole first page of the quality procedures manual. It will make the underlying structure of your organisation available at a glance and be easy to refer back to.

### *Drawing a diagram of management processes*

Another very effective way of presenting an overview of your organisation's management processes is to use a diagram. Management processes along the same time-line can be shown as a chain of interlocking events. Supporting management processes can be shown as a series of separate activities (see Figure 23).

▲ To connect these processes to the procedures later on, you can use a numbering system.
**Company D: Management process**
*1 Business management*
1.1 Development/ engineering
1.2 Sales enquiry
1.3 Sales order processing
1.4 Materials control

## Quality management procedures

Now you are ready for the main business of the quality procedures manual – the procedures. The procedures are there to tell people how to carry out all the management activities that

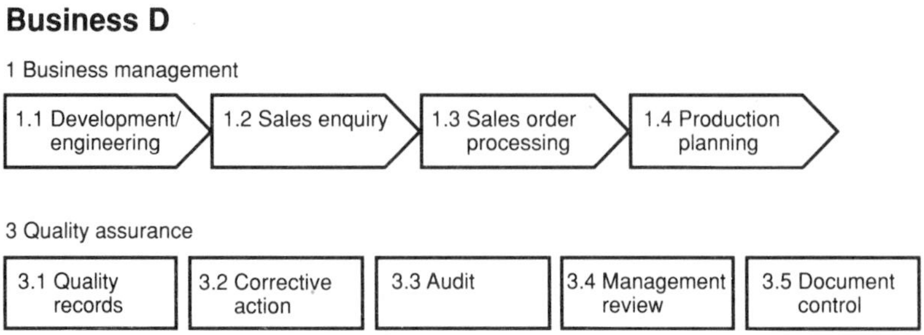

**Business D**

1 Business management

| 1.1 Development/ engineering | 1.2 Sales enquiry | 1.3 Sales order processing | 1.4 Production planning |

3 Quality assurance

| 3.1 Quality records | 3.2 Corrective action | 3.3 Audit | 3.4 Management review | 3.5 Document control |

**Figure 23** *Drawing a diagram of management processes*

need to be done in the organisation. Don't go overboard in trying to specify everything to the last detail. The procedures are simply there to make sure that across the organisation people do things in the same way, and in a way which fits with how other people are working. The procedures aren't job descriptions and they won't take the place of experience, common sense or on-the-job training. Anything that could be described as fine detail will simply add weight to the procedures manual without adding value to the organisation.

## *Developing the content of the procedures*

The quality manual procedures must say:

- how all management activities are to be carried out
- who will carry out the activities (using job titles rather than individual names)
- how the activities are to be documented
- the workplace instructions which will be needed for reference.

Think along the time-line about what happens to your customers' orders. Ask questions like:

- how do we process a customer enquiry?
- how do we confirm an order?
- how do we schedule the order?
- how do we organise the resources to meet the order?
- how do we review the order?

- how do we decide on order completion?

- how do we get paid?

Putting together the content of the procedures will involve collecting a lot of information which is there already, as well as developing procedures where there are gaps, or documentation systems where existing practices don't use them. You will have to research and test both old and new procedures before you can really judge what needs to be in the manual in the first place, what needs to be emphasised, or what needs to be given less prominence.

Drafting procedures isn't something that can be done piece-meal during odd moments. Good procedures take time and effort to get right. They will present you with the biggest communication challenge of all: how to ensure that what you meant when you wrote them is what is actually understood – the case study at the end of this chapter is a good example of that particular problem. The only way you can be sure of dealing effectively with this potential minefield is to test and check the procedures as you write them with the people who are going to be using them. They will soon tell you if you've got it wrong.

It really would be very unwise to go straight to the final version of your procedures, without having tried them out first.

There are examples of procedures in the Appendix. The information given in the quality procedures manual is summarised in Figure 24.

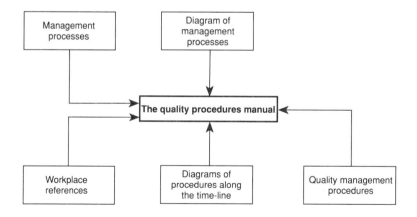

**Figure 24** *A summary of information for the quality procedures manual*

# Guidelines for writing procedures

**The format**

*Title*
This covers the subject of the procedure

*Scope*
This clarifies the title and describes who is affected by it

*Responsibilities*
These should be clearly defined either separately or within the procedure

*References*
You should list all the support documentation which you refer to in the procedure. You may need to reference generic rather than specific support documentation, eg test specifications

*Flow chart*
Not compulsory, but a good way of giving an overview of the procedure

**The content**

- use job titles, not names
- refer to forms, tools, and technical items by their official names to avoid confusion
- define any unique or special terms and abbreviations

**The style**

- be clear
- be concise
- follow the logical sequence of events
- check for any ambiguity

## Postscript: revisiting the quality policy manual

When your procedures are all finally written down, you will be ready to revisit the last section of the quality policy manual, to fill in the chart showing how your procedures conform to the requirements of the quality standard. This will be an important checking process for you: it will close the circle, and highlight:

- any areas which your procedures do not cover

- any areas where your procedures are incomplete

- any areas where they do not match the standard and where you haven't explained why.

You may also have to review your organisation chart to make sure that the responsibilities you have allocated in the procedures are reflected in the chart, and vice versa.

Carry out this check thoroughly – don't leave anything to chance.

# Case Study

## Heelands Construction Ltd – Using Procedures Effectively

Heelands was a traditional manufacturer making a timber product which was sometimes sold direct to the public, but more often direct to the building trade. Turnover in 1983/84 was approaching £35 million. With its product known as top of the range, the company had a justifiable pride in itself.

Heelands was part of a large international group. It was based on three sites and had a product range which went from small standard items produced in their thousands to specialist products manufactured in tens or even as one-off special items. Two of the factories had large production lines which were able to cut, assemble and finish the timber product. As well as the main production lines, each of these two sites had a small area set aside for special orders. The third factory was dedicated to special orders and short run items.

At the beginning of 1984, Heelands decided to prepare for BS5750 registration. At this time, BS5750 was in its early days. It had been applied extensively to the metal manufacturing industry, but timber was an unknown application. The timber industry also had quite a different culture from the metal-working industry, as was to become apparent.

The quality management consultant whom Heelands appointed to lead the project, Phil Brown, was very interested in developing the application of the BS5750 standard in this way. However, as he sat in the factory manager's office on the Monday morning when the project began, problems began to come to light. Phil was explaining the principles of the quality management standard and its basic requirements. He began to talk in general terms about goods-inward inspection and the need to check that what the supplier had supplied met Heelands' needs. As he did so, he was surprised to see the factory manager's expression change from one of interest to one of disbelief. Half an hour later it became clear why.

First of all, the industry had no usable timber specifications which would enable them to assess the incoming materials. Although international grading rules were in existence, they were biased towards the needs of the supplying saw mills, not the manufacturing customer. The industry prided itself on the knowledge of its staff and relied on the experience and expertise of individuals to grade timber as it came in.

The next problem was that no supplier records were kept. And it would have been impossible to say which timber had come from a particular supplier in any case since there was no system to identify or trace it.

Heelands relied instead on a global measure of timber yield. They knew what went into the factory and what went out. By carrying out monthly work-in-progress stock checks they could see what had been partly converted and calculate the yield.

Formal identification of types of timber wasn't necessary as it was traditional for the craftsmen to go into the stockyard and select whatever they wanted whenever they wanted. They didn't need to be told what the wood was, they could tell by looking at it.

This was only the start. As Phil discovered more about Heelands, the same kinds of issues were repeated everywhere he looked. For example, not only were there no specifications for materials, but there were also no specifications for products. Heelands craftsmen didn't use drawings for their products – they made them to traditional patterns that were passed on from one worker to another. There were no definitions of the product base anywhere that Phil could see.

The list of negatives grew ever longer. No production route cards, no formal inspection, none of the basic infrastructure needed to start building a system. Phil realised that even to introduce the most basic controls would be a huge change management exercise.

In the next few days Phil spent most of his time with the production manager, explaining to him what controls were needed and enlisting his whole-hearted support. They decided to start by working on three issues:

- defining the materials

- defining the product specifications and production methods

- defining procedures.

Defining the materials proved to be quite a challenge for Phil. At first he suggested that they define the materials by thinking about what the buyers were looking for when they purchased the timber. But after hours of fruitless discussion they abandoned this idea. It was impossible to get agreement.

Phil then tried to identify the objective characteristics of the wood which would form a basis for its specification: things such as

- colour

- grain

- pattern of the wood.

But again, this approach ran into problems. It was impossible to define the characteristics of the wood in a way which would work for everyone.

Then, late one night, as Phil sat with the production manager wearily poring over piles of international grading rules, the penny suddenly dropped.

Grading in the timber industry didn't go by consistent quality specifications. Nature wasn't consistent: two equally 'good' pieces of timber would have quite different characteristics. What the craftsmen were judging when they appraised a piece of timber was the number of defects. So quality actually depended on the number and size of defects.

With a real sense of progress, Phil made a note to redefine the BS5750 requirements for specification and measurement. In metal manufacturing industries materials would be measured in terms of what was good about them – their composition and tolerances, for example. In the timber industry, however, quality would be measured by the specification and measurement of defects.

Phil then moved on to look at product specifications and production methods. This was a very long, painstaking process. It took twelve months just to log every single family of products, every single item of production, and every single production method, manual and machine. Phil discovered that the same products were actually being made differently in each of the three factories – and that there were huge variations in material usage between the factories. When he mentioned this to the sales department, there was an immediate reaction. The sales staff had long been puzzled by the difference in customer satisfaction with one of their products – some customers were very happy, while others complained.

With the specifications complete, it was then time to move into the stockyard and the shop floor. Stockyard procedures consisting of first-in first-out controls were introduced. Heelands began to log supplier deliveries and to calculate yields by supplier. This had quite a dramatic effect. After 18 months of calculating supplier yields, Heelands dropped their second largest supplier whose yields were consistently poor.

Formal inspection checks by the operators were introduced and different production rates were monitored. The materials that went into the production process were counted at the start, reducing the need for monthly stock checks.

Resistance did occur. One supervisor held out against the new systems for 18 months, preferring to rely on his own notebooks which took 5 hours every day to complete. Other staff were prone to mutter 'that's not the way we do things'. But gradually the change began to take hold. The benefits were too obvious to deny.

There was one unexpected benefit. As the procedures spread through more and more of the organisation, they uncovered a major fraud. Phil couldn't believe it at first, but the evidence was there. It transpired that for many years scrap material had been signed out as firewood. This was quite legitimate. But the new systems measured scrap levels and revealed that they were unexpectedly high. There was one good piece of timber in each bundle. The production manager began marking the components with security markers. Then the police, with ultraviolet lights in the garage of the ring leader, were able to do the rest.

# Workplace References 6

## The purpose of workplace references

Workplace references are informational materials which employees need to use to do their jobs properly (see Figure 25). These are the materials which, before you have ISO9000 registration, are never where you think they are when you want them. So you either spend valuable and frustrating time trying to track them down, or trying to remember roughly what was in them, or do without. People can be very ingenious about finding ways to do their jobs without proper information. They will ask their colleagues, or photocopy something similar, or make more or less intelligent guesses. But the ISO9000 requirement to identify exactly what reference materials people are going to need and where they are kept means that your organisation will become much more efficient at locating and using information and also much more effective, because the information people use will be correct (see section 4.5.1 of ISO9001).

**Figure 25** *Workplace references relate to the bottom level of the organisation*

Workplace references might seem initially to be in the same category as the tools, materials, designs and equipment which management provides to employees to enable them to deliver goods or services, as informational tools of the trade. Viewed in this way, workplace references are a pragmatic rather than a strategic concern. However, once you start to plan out what information your organisation needs to support its key activities, you will quickly find yourself moving from purely practical considerations, such as what technical manuals you need to have and where you are going to put them, to thinking about what information would actually enhance the quality of the jobs people do. In this way, workplace references can play a strategic role in your organisation's quality system.

## The audience for workplace references

Anyone who has tasks to perform will need to use workplace references, either regularly or from time to time. The ISO9000 requirement is to make the materials people need accessible by classifying and indexing them and putting them where they can be found. People have a strong tendency to make assumptions and an antipathy to checking: the standard can help to change this culture, where it exists, by making checking easier than guessing. Flexibility is also an important benefit of implementing the standard, as knowledge is not confined to individuals. Anyone can find out what they need to know from the system, without having to rely on particular individuals.

A key audience for the workplace references consists of newcomers to the organisation, or those who are in charge of their training. Workplace references will help to minimise the learning curves newcomers go through as they find out how things are done, and make sure good habits are formed.

## Workplace references and the quality management manual

Within the quality procedures manual, you will have identified workplace references that are needed to carry out particular procedures. In a small organisation, you may not have many workplace references. In this case, you may choose to put copies of the references in the manual.

However, in the majority of cases the volume and the detail will make this impossible. What you can do in the final part of the quality management manual is to provide a catalogue or index to them. The workplace references section of the quality management manual will tell the user:

- what types of workplace references are available

- how they are controlled (their *status*)

- where they are stored (their *location*)

- how they can be accessed.

## Types of workplace references

Workplace references can either be generated internally by the content of your work and the processes you use, or externally by the influence which people outside your organisation exert over what you do and how you do it.

## Internally generated workplace references

Most of the workplace references will be generated by your own internal processes. They will specify how key operations of your organisation, and of your quality management system, should be carried out, so that individual people can do their jobs to the required standard. Remember to identify carefully first what these key operations are. Unless you are selective, you will find yourself bogged down in drawing up specifications for details which won't make any real difference to your business objectives: in other words, which don't need specifying.

▲ *Specify:* key operations.
*Don't specify:* background operations.

For example, let's assume that in one or more areas of your business your staff use computers. Obvious workplace references will be software manuals. Then you will probably develop checklists to cover housekeeping and maintenance tasks to make sure the computer system operates effectively. You could go further and specify how files and folders should be organised, how files should be named and how different versions of the same document should be labelled. All these things are admittedly desirable but only version control is likely to have a direct influence on your business efficiency, and then only if work is shared between different members of staff or different departments.

### Examples of internally generated workplace references

Examples of workplace references that are generated internally are:

* forms

* technical manuals

* technical instructions

* technical drawings

* instructions and checklists

* internal specifications and standards

* methodologies for testing

* reference and research materials.

◆ Company A
Procedure 3.2
Classifying orders
3.2.1 Sort orders into payment categories
3.2.2 Check order prices against the alarm list. The alarm list is produced by the Customer Services Manager. It highlights all non-standard prices.
3.2.3 Send a list of orders and their categories to Accounts.
**Use the List 70 form.**

*Forms*   Forms of some kind are an indispensable part of every system. They can be paper or electronic, off-the-shelf or custommade. What they have in common is the collection and transfer of information from one part of your organisation to another.

The principle of selectivity is particularly important when it comes to forms: remember that it is the experience of every bureaucracy that forms multiply through time.

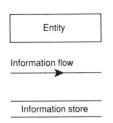

**Figure 26** *Data flow notation*

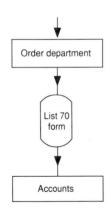

**Figure 27** *The data flow diagram*

One starting point for considering what forms are needed in your organisation is the quality procedures. These will tell you when information transfers have to take place. You can then think about how each transfer will be made and recorded.

You might also find it useful to use a data flow diagram for an overview of how information is moving around the organisation. Data flow diagrams are used by the computer industry to plan networks and are governed by particular rules and conventions. If you are interested in developing a detailed information model of this kind for your company, you should look up the methodology in a specialist book or bring in outside expertise.

However, without being an expert you can develop a helpful model yourself by adopting the general principles of data modelling. Data modelling works by identifying firstly entities, that is things (either people or departments or even buildings) which information moves between. These will appear as boxes on your diagram.

Information moving between entities is represented by lines carrying directional arrows.

When information stops moving, it is held in an information store: a filing cabinet, or a computer file, or a computer database. An information store can be shown by parallel lines (see Figure 26).

Finally, you can look at how information will be transferred from one place to another. Concentrate on those transfers which will require a form to carry them out. You can show how information is transferred by using a lozenge shape on the line of the information flow, and by writing the method of transfer in the lozenge.

The whole diagram will show you how information is moving around. You can then check each information transfer to make sure that you can control it, if necessary, by a form (see Figure 27).

*Instruction manuals* Instruction manuals are another very common kind of workplace reference. Like forms, they can be hard copy or electronic, off-the-shelf or custom-made. They will normally explain how equipment or processes work and include guidance on the design, installation or maintenance of equipment.

Ideally the manuals themselves will be presented in a clear and accessible way, user-centred and well designed, so that people can actually use them. However, computer manuals, for example, can still be rather product-led, concentrating on the product rather than on the needs of the user. If parts of your organisation are relying on manuals which are still poorly written and presented, it is worth seeing what you can do about the problem, so that you get the benefits from standardising practices and not just the frustrations. The same rule that applies to the quality management manual applies to technical manuals: if they aren't usable, they won't be used. If your organisation is large enough, it may be able to specify how its technical manuals must be written, as the Post Office did in 1989.

*Instructions and checklists*  Instructions and checklists add detail to particular procedures. They can cover such diverse things as the layout of letters, how to answer the telephone, how to leave a machine at the end of the day, or what to look for in deliveries from suppliers. Instructions and checklists can be effective at quite a high level: for example, it would be entirely appropriate for a senior professional to use a checklist as a prompt when taking a brief from a client.

♦ Checklist for typesetters:
[ ] Colour naming
[ ] Page settings
[ ] EPSs
[ ] Tint screen dpi
[ ] Tint percentage
[ ] Fonts
[ ] Data files

*Internal specifications and standards*  Defining these is very important for your quality system. Setting specifications and standards translates the objectives of the quality policy statement into reality. Specifications and standards may be influenced to some degree by external factors, such as industry norms and standards, but as long as you comply with any external constraints, it is much more to the point to set your own. Nor will these be fixed standards. Japanese companies have shown that it is possible to continuously improve specifications and standards and so to keep ahead of the market.

♦ Specification for a side salad:
3 lettuce leaves
2 tablespoons salad dressing
1 teaspoon raisins
4 2mm slices cucumber
4 2mm slices beetroot

*Testing methods*  These will specify what methods you are using to test equipment or products and how to analyse test data. These methods will support the quality standards and specifications you have set, by stating how you intend to measure conformance. You may well find that there are statistically-based methodologies, such as distribution curves (see Figure 28), which you would like to use, but which nobody knows how to apply. This should lead to training programmes, not to a reduction in appropriate testing techniques.

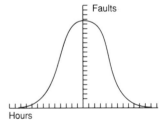

**Figure 28** *A normal distribution*

*Reference and research materials*  These are materials which will enhance and develop the work that people do. They could include trade publications, periodicals, market research reports technical research reports and so on. Your company will be able to put together its own list of relevant reference and research materials. These materials will build up a great deal of information over time and make sure your organisation keeps up to date.

♦ An example of reference and research for a company in the fashion industry:
Drapers Record
MINTEL retail reports
The Fabric Book

## Externally generated workplace references

By externally generated workplace references we mean the laws, standards and guidelines set by bodies which are outside your organisation, but which influence aspects of what you do. Examples of externally generated workplace references are:

- legislation
- industry standards, codes of practice and trade association guidelines
- customer specifications
- National Vocational Qualifications work instructions.

### Legislation

◆ Common types of legislation are: Health and safety legislation Fire regulations Building regulations Care Of Substances Hazardous to Health Employee liability insurance.

Keeping within legislation is clearly a prerequisite to operating at all, with or without a quality system. The quality system means that you should not be caught out. At the outset, make sure that you know what legislation effects you and that you conform to it. You must then make sure that you have a system for keeping your information up to date. You don't have to have bad intentions to fall foul of legislation: ignorance will do just as well.

Some legislation is common to all industries. Other legislation is industry specific. The food, toy, transport or construction industries, for example, are tightly governed by particular legislation in the interests of public safety.

### Industry standards, codes of practice and trade association guidelines

◆ Examples of standards are: Law Society codes of practice, Institute of Chartered Accountants guidelines, Press Council guidelines.

Trade and industry guidelines are not legally binding but they have official status, and if you want to be known as a quality organisation you will want to conform to them. Often you can signal conformance by becoming a member of societies or associations. Make sure you are up to date with codes of practice and guidelines, and that you regularly check conformance.

### Customer specifications

Customer specifications can be either for products or processes. They are common in the motor industry, for example, where particular products have to be specified to fit in with a central design, and where the quality of the products is ensured by the specification of quality assurance systems.

There can be a problem of control with customer specifications. Although they originate with the customer, they need to be owned and controlled by your own internal processes. For example, if the customer specification changes, your change control procedures must apply.

### National Vocational Qualifications work instructions

The National Vocational Qualifications (NVQ) scheme has some significant implications for quality management systems at the workplace reference level.

The National Council for Vocational Qualifications (NCVQ) was established in 1986 to work with industry lead bodies to develop a nationally coherent framework of vocational qualifications. Eleven occupational categories have been identified. The NCVQ's objective is ultimately to identify five levels of NVQs in each occupational area. The NVQ framework from Level 1 to Level 4 will be completed by 1992: 250 have already been established. Level 1 is the simplest level, covering tasks such as unloading frozen food from a refrigerated lorry. At the other end of the scale, Level 5 will include professional qualifications. As individuals work towards achieving NVQs at each level, they put together their own National Record of Achievement (NRA), which is a personal portfolio of achievements and qualifications.

The interesting thing about NVQs is that, although they represent qualifications which are transferable across industries in the same way as traditional qualifications, they are not based on standardised examinations but on a mixture of work experience and training or examinations. In order to standardise work experience, NVQs are based on detailed workplace instructions. So, if an employee has reached Level 1 in office skills, for example, an employer can know from consulting the relevant NVQ workplace instructions exactly how that person has been taught to answer the telephone, set up a filing system and so on.

The implication is that, if you want to be an NVQ employer and provide training to NVQ standards for your employees, you will have to adopt these externally developed workplace instructions within your organisation.

There are definite advantages:

- all the development work for the workplace instructions is done for you, by experts in the same industry

- you have a ready-made training programme for staff

- recruiting from other NVQ trainees will cut down the learning curve for new staff, since they will know how things are done.

Of course there will be work involved in becoming an NVQ organisation, but it is certainly something to put at least on your medium- to long-term agenda. In time NVQs will become transferable throughout Europe, standardising work practices in the process.

For more information about NVQs, contact the National Council for Vocational Qualifications, 222 Euston Road, London NW1 2BZ.

◆ NVQ occupational categories are:
1. Tending animals and plants
2. Extracting and providing natural resources
3. Construction
4. Engineering
5. Manufacturing
6. Transportation
7. Providing goods and services
8. Providing health, social care and professional services
9. Providing business services
10. Communicating
11. Developing and extending knowledge and skill.

## Keeping workplace references up to date

Identifying and installing workplace references is a one-off task. You will then need to make sure key items, such as legislation or industry guidelines, are kept up to date. There is no easy way to do this, unless your industry has developed an information monitoring service you can use. Libraries can also offer a current awareness service suitable for large organisations. But if you do not have these options, you will have to keep aware of what is happening by reading the national press and any relevant trade journals.

## Status and location

ISO9000 requires you to be able to give the status and location of all workplace references. This requirement is the practical heart of the matter, as if you don't meet it, you may know what you should have but you still won't be able to find it.

The easiest way of fulfilling this requirement, and indeed the most logical way of organising your workplace reference materials, is to set up a library system. Librarianship is a discipline in its own right and you should consult an expert if you have very extensive plans.

The kind of system you end up with will depend on:

- how you produce or are supplied with material

- the amount of material to be accessed

- the importance of the material

- your own resources.

### The library system matrix

The library system matrix (see Figure 29) looks at two key variables, the amount of material in the workplace references and the importance of the material to the main functions of your organisation. Suggestions are given for the type of library system which might be appropriate in each of the quadrants. Of course, most organisations will have a mixture of materials, some bulky, some important, some less so. The matrix suggests which approach to use for the majority of the information you hold.

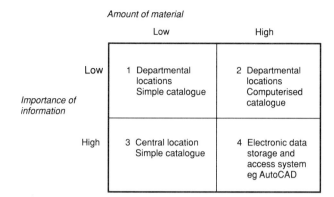

**Figure 29** *The library system matrix*

## First quadrant: Low amount, low importance

Your organisation will be in this quadrant if you use relatively few workplace references, and if any references which are used are not critically important to key business operations.

◆ Examples of companies who might be in the first quadrant:
Small retailers
Office cleaning company
Ice-cream van

Any system for organising these materials should be kept quite simple. You probably won't need more than some cupboard and shelf space and an index list. If you have a computer, set up a simple database as a catalogue, but a manual index will also be quite feasible.

## Second quadrant: High amount, low importance

Your organisation will be in this quadrant if it would benefit from access to a wide range of reference materials, but does not rely on them for key business functions.

◆ Typical organisations in the second quadrant might be:
Service companies
Design studios
Research and development departments

Because there is a lot of material to be controlled, you will really need to use a computer-based library program. There are a number of these on the market which allow you to build up a database of the materials you have, and to search for them in a number of ways, for example by key words.

Or you could choose a non-specialist database program and enter the details of new materials as they arrive. A computer system will make the control of materials much easier and also make access much quicker.

If you have a lot of material, you will obviously need to find space for it. You should consider storing information electronically wherever possible to save space – on a computer hard disk or on an optical disk, for example.

You can probably find enough physical space if materials are distributed throughout the building. However, be careful not to let materials become absorbed into departmental libraries, with each department making its own collection of forms, instructions, manuals, journals, books and so on. Although this approach keeps information close to the workplace, experience shows that isolated departmental libraries are in fact not very effective. From the quality management point of view, they are certainly difficult to control. From a policy point of view, they do not promote the integration of information or give an overview of information resources in the organisation. In reality, they just tend to get lost.

### Third quadrant: Low amount, high importance

◆ Typical industries in this quadrant might be:
Catering
Toy making
Transport

Your organisation will be in this quadrant if there is not a large quantity of workplace reference material, but what there is is vitally important to the business. Industries which are heavily regulated by legislation or industry sector guidelines are likely to fall into this category.

Workplace references in this situation need to be carefully and centrally controlled and located. How you choose to do this will depend on your resources. Because you are not dealing with large amounts of material a manual system is a viable option.

### Fourth quadrant: High amount, high importance

◆ Typical industries in this quadrant might be:
Nuclear installations
Aircraft manufacture
Construction
Pharmaceutical companies

Finally, you may work in an organisation which uses very large quantities of workplace reference material, all of which is vital to the success of the product or process.

For all these companies, it is vitally important for public safety reasons to hold detailed instructions and specifications at every level of their processes. Also for organisations like, for example, British Nuclear Fuels or military installations, there is a particularly important requirement to be able to access volumes of maintenance and emergency information very quickly.

These organisations rely on sophisticated and powerful computer packages. In the North Sea oil industry, CAD (Computer Aided Design) packages such as Drawbase can create and store drawings of each rig, along with specifications of the materials used and maintenance needed. Any objects in the rigs can also be recorded. If the rooms and these objects are bar-coded, their position can be checked out with a hand-held computer and any changes spotted immediately.

In other industries, the most sophisticated information storage and retrieval systems now use optical disks and multi-media applications. Optical disks have the advantage of speed. Multi-media applications mean that pictures, videos and voice messages can be stored, as well as text. This is an important development for maintenance and emergency instructions, as a multi-media application can actually show you what to do and how to do it. Even if you are a comparatively small company, and can't afford or don't need such state-of-the-art information technology, you should think carefully about how a more intermediate technology can help you if you need to control a high volume of important information.

## Beyond Level 3

Much of the information held by systems in the fourth quadrant of the library system matrix actually goes beyond the initial requirement of the ISO9000 quality management standard – into what we might call Level 4 and beyond.

Take for example a company which manufactures DIY products, such as fillers, grouts, wallpaper paste and strippers. At Level 3, workplace references will be about how to mix products. Quantities, materials, temperatures and processes will all be specified. This information will be enough to ensure the consistency and quality of each product line.

However, the products in the mixes are made up from a large number of formulas which also have to be specified. This information, vital to the quality of the final products, operates at one remove from the workplace, at what we might call Level 4. In order to develop its formulas, the company also needs to hold substantive databases containing accepted chemistry, research and reference materials. This information at two removes from the workplace, still directly relevant to the core business, is really at Level 5.

As you look at the reference material which supports your organisation, you may well see how you could develop your library system beyond Level 3. You will probably not have to do this for ISO9000 in the first instance. However, the system you set up to control your Level 3 workplace references will give you the framework to develop materials over time, in a programme of continuous improvement.

## Creating a guide to workplace references

The third part of the quality management manual serves as a guide to whatever library system you have, whether it is a shelf and a card index, or a complex computer-based application. This section of the quality management manual might contain:

- the business objectives of the workplace references

- the kinds of materials and information involved
- information about how to access materials
- copies of workplace references, where appropriate.

### The business objectives of the workplace references

In this section you can show how the reference material you hold underpins the quality management of key business operations.

### The kinds of materials and information involved

Here you need to set out the categories of reference materials you hold, such as forms, manuals, industry magazines and so on. If you have used a classification system to organise your materials, you should list the classification headings here.

### How to access materials

You should explain here the system you have for accessing materials. You don't have to give all the details of how your system works – just an overview, which will guide potential users in the right direction.

### Copies of reference materials, where appropriate

It may be appropriate in some cases to include actual examples of forms or other short reference documents such as instructions in the manual itself. This may help the user to work out what reference material is needed and how to use it. However, this idea needs to be used sparingly. The quality management manual is not the place to collect together large amounts of workplace references.

What this section will do is direct users to materials which will protect and enhance their competence in the roles they perform. For anyone involved in the core productive activities, the workplace references are likely to be the most helpful and significant part of the manual.

## Relating the workplace references to the quality procedures manual

Finally, remember that the quality procedures manual should refer to workplace references whenever they form part of the procedures. You will need to check the two parts of the manual carefully to make sure that they correspond.

All the information about workplace references is summarised in Figure 30.

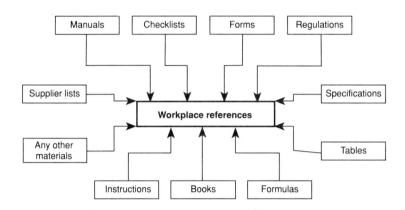

**Figure 30** *Information for workplace references*

## Case Study

### Alldis Information – Improving the Knowledge Base

Alldis Information grew rapidly throughout the 1980s. It was one of the new service industries of the decade which exploited the availability of electronic information. Alldis provided an on-line information service 12 hours a day. Alldis customers would call in with requests for information and expect to have a response within half an hour at the most.

When the customer's request came in, the telephone operator who took the call would immediately pass on the request to a PC operator, who would then start to search the appropriate databases. The customer would then receive either a fax of the information print-out or a phone call. The search was timed automatically and an invoice sent on to the customer. There was a two-stage payment system. If the search took up to 15 minutes, it was charged at the lower rate of £11.40. Any search over 15 minutes was charged at the higher rate of £20.60.

By 1990 Alldis had 45 PCs and 120 telephone lines. Demand for information was heavy, in spite of the recession. In fact, the recession was good for the company, as it became more and more necessary for suppliers and contractors to check each other out. For example, a supplier could lose thousands of pounds by supplying a company in trouble: on the other hand, it was important not to turn away good business. In these circumstances, £11.40 was not a lot to pay.

However, when Alldis's accountant Richard Hughes analysed the end-of-year returns for 1990 he saw that the profitability of the company had fallen to 4 per cent over the year. When the company had first started, it had been achieving margins of about 11 per cent. Really, thought Hughes, margins should have improved over the years rather than deteriorated. Overheads were spread more widely and costs had been very steady. In fact, the cost of the electronic equipment Alldis used had actually fallen over this period by up to 6 per cent, including the volume discounts Alldis could now demand.

Hughes discussed his findings with the board of Alldis Information. No one knew why this had happened. The finance director was confident that the charging scale they used was correct. Finally it was agreed that Hughes should be employed for a week's consultancy to see if he could find out what was happening.

Hughes started his research with an open mind. He was introduced to the employees of the company as a student doing research. Although there was some scepticism about this, and some open suspicion that he might be a 'time and motion man', he was able to sit in with the operators quite freely and talk to them about their jobs.

Hughes quickly learned to respect the speed and efficiency of the staff as they worked long hours processing a wide variety of requests. However, he quickly also picked up the fact that people were working in an atmosphere of tension and frustration, brought about by the equipment they were using. It seemed that every piece of technology had its own idiosyncrasies. As he watched, he began to keep a log of the problems he saw. Typical entries read like this:

| Time | Work station no | Problem | Solution | Time taken |
|------|------|---------|----------|------|
| 9.20 | 4 | Computer crashes when trying to open database | Re-booted × 3 | 15 mins |
| 9.21 | 25 | Computer very slow | None | 10 mins |
| 9.45 | 18 | Problems transferring phone call | Kept trying | 3 mins |
| 9.52 | 33 | Computer giving error message | Re-booted × 1 | 5 mins |
| 9.56 | 4 | Print-out problems: paper stuck | Re-loaded | 5 mins |
| 10.02 | 7 | Computer crashing | Re-booted × 4 | 20 mins |
| 10.05 | 22 | Phone transfer problem | Telephonist walked to work station | 5 mins |

Hughes noted that:

- problems were happening at almost all work stations

- everyone used the computer programs in slightly different ways

- there was no strategy for solving problems apart from trying the application again; mostly this succeeded but it could take a lot of time

- operators at the switchboard and at the PCs did not know why problems were occurring

- in over 90 per cent of cases, equipment problems pushed the job over the 15 minute limit. However, in all these cases the lower rate was charged to the client, because the operators felt that the time the problems took could not fairly be passed on

- operators did not pass on details of their problems to management. They felt responsible for them, and had encountered the attitude that if they were doing their job properly they would not experience them. Management based this assumption on the claims the manufacturers made about how the systems would work

- there was no one with any expertise in networking or phone systems in the organisation.

Hughes showed the log he had made, and his observations, to a colleague who had considerable knowledge of computer network systems. His friend immediately identified several probable causes of the problems. For example, crashes were happening when someone tried to access a database which was already in use. The first user would slow down while this was happening. Phone transfers were similarly affected when a particular line was overloaded.

Hughes' friend could not believe that Alldis was living with these problems on a day-to-day basis. He began to explain to Hughes what should be done about them. Hughes stopped him, however. He didn't need to know the details of solutions just yet. His job was to persuade the board that it was asking for trouble to base the business on a technology which no one really understood or could maintain. They were trusting to chance and paying heavily for their lack of knowledge.

Hughes outlined a plan for the board. The whole system needed to be evaluated by an expert. Then workplace instructions should be written and kept by each work station. There should be a section in these instructions about what to do when particular problems were encountered. All staff should be trained from this manual, so that they had a common frame of reference and a common approach to solving problems.

The company should also either appoint a maintenance engineer or take out a maintenance agreement.

In this way, they could regain their profit margins which were being swallowed up by wasted time.

# Part 3 Writing and Designing the Quality Management Manual

# Writing the Quality Management Manual 7

## The importance of style

Getting the content of the quality management manual right will be a big task in itself. You may well feel that, in the context of all the other work you have had to do, worrying about the niceties of style is really the icing on the cake, the last thing on the agenda. And of course, although your manual may fail its desktop check by the quality management assessor if its content is incomplete, it won't fail if the assessor doesn't like your prose style.

But if your users don't like your prose style, if they can't follow what you mean, or work out how sections of the manual relate to what they know of their organisation, the chances are that they will not use the manual at all, or at the very least not use it correctly. It is worth repeating that the most common reason for companies not to succeed in gaining registration to quality management standards is that what their manual says and what their people do are not consistent: in other words, because the manual is not being used properly. Of course you can't persuade people to use the manual if they are determined not to. What you can do is to make sure that there are no barriers to understanding in the way that you have written and presented it. In this way, the style of the manual will contribute as much to the success of your implementation programme as its content.

## Rules for writing

Over the years, technical writers have gained some useful insights into how best to write complex informational material. The rest of this chapter will look at some of these insights, expressed as rules which you can use to check out how easy your work is to understand. The assumption underlying all the rules is that the reader will be working hard to master the content of what is being said, and will find any obscurities or difficulties in written style a barrier to this understanding.

Rules for clear writing can be divided into rules for words, and rules for language structure. But remember that in reality the way you write will be a mixture of both. For example, if you find you need to change the vocabulary you have used, you will very often find yourself changing the sentence structure as well.

## Rules for words

This section is about the basic unit of language – words: how to choose them and how to use them.

### *Use common words*

◆

| Officialese | Common words |
|---|---|
| aforementioned | mentioned before |
| in conjunction with | along with |
| prior to | before |
| precis | summary |
| retained | kept |
| with regard to | about |
| via | by, through |
| actuate | start |
| personnel | people/staff |

When you start to write the quality management manual, you will be aware of its importance and its official status, and you will probably find yourself adopting a formal and official tone, characterised by formal and official words. Most of the official communications we receive are still couched in 'officialese', in spite of the movement in recent years towards using clear English for such documents. It will not be surprising if your model, conscious or unconscious, of how to write proper formal documents has long sentences and weighty words.

There is no reason at all why you should not use common, straightforward words throughout the quality management manual: in fact there is every reason to do so. Your users should not have to spend unnecessary time and energy puzzling over, or being distracted by, words which they don't really recognise, or don't quite understand.

A useful way to check the vocabulary you are using is to imagine speaking what you are writing. If you wouldn't say it to a colleague, you shouldn't write it.

### *Limit the number of words you use*

◆

| Long phrases | Shorter phrases |
|---|---|
| as a result of | because of |
| by means of | by |
| each and every | every |
| inasmuch as | since |
| in order that | so that |

You may be tempted to use a lot of words, as well as weighty ones, to make your quality management manual authoritative. However, quantities of words will effectively disguise your meaning. It is a well-known fact that often writers who are not clear about what they are saying will try to disguise their confusion by using lots of words to talk round the issue rather than tackling it direct. And remember that more words to read mean more work for the reader to do.

One area where extra and unnecessary words can creep in is that of common phrases. Many contain extra words which don't mean anything and just add length. This is an easy point to check.

## Explain technical terms

We looked at the problem of how to present technical terms to do with quality management to a mixed audience in Chapter 4, *The Quality Policy Manual*.

The technical terms you will want to use in the procedures manual will be work related: abbreviations, proprietary terms or industry references. Your audience will be familiar with a good number of these terms; certainly you don't have the problem of addressing experts and novices together, as you had in the policy manual.

However, remember that one important purpose of the quality procedures manual is to introduce new staff to your organisation and how it works. New staff will probably have some knowledge of technical terms which are common to the industry, but you should be careful to provide explanations of anything which might cause difficulty.

There are a number of options for providing explanations of technical terms:

* a glossary at the end of each section of the quality management manual

* footnotes

* explanations after the term.

## Glossaries

Glossaries are useful catch-all devices, which allow you to provide detailed explanations of terms without disrupting the flow of the main text. However, glossaries can be rather hit or miss from your readers' perspective:

◆ **Be wary of false friends**
*Text*
Clean timber will be charged at the higher rate
*Glossary*
**clean timber** – timber which is free of knots

* they may find it awkward to leaf backwards and forwards and underuse the glossary

* they may not find the words they want and stop looking

* most confusingly, they may meet some false friends (also known as *faux amis*). These are terms which seem to have an obvious meaning, which might not, however, be the meaning you intended or the meaning your organisation uses. In these cases, your readers won't bother to look up what they think they already know, and your glossary won't be effective.

*Writing and designing*

## *Footnotes*

◆ **Footnotes**
Clean timber [1] will be charged at the higher rate.

_____

[1] timber which is free of knots

To create footnotes, simply number the terms you want to explain and provide explanations for them in small print at the bottom of the page. Footnotes have the advantage of keeping explanations on the same page, so that the reader only has to look down for the information rather than turning over a number of pages.

In narrative texts, the normal rule for editors is to use a footnote only the first time a term is used and assume that the reader will remember the meaning the next time it occurs. This keeps the page relatively free of annotations.

The quality management manual is not a narrative text, however. You can't assume that your readers are working through the procedures sequentially and picking up all first-time explanations. On the contrary, the procedures will invariably be used as a reference source for specific activities. So you may have to give each term a footnote explanation every time it appears.

## *Explanations after the term*

◆ **Explanations of abbreviations**
A WDR (written data request) must be answered immediately. Write the MFN (manufacturer number) on the box. Complete and send the FOC (free of charge) order.

An alternative to footnotes is to include explanations of technical terms in brackets immediately after the term. If your readers are familiar with the term, they can pass over the bracketed explanation. Readers who need the explanation don't have to do any work at all to find out what they need to know.

You will have to decide whether or not to repeat the explanation every time the term is used. This can be rather clumsy, but it might be necessary for the reasons we discussed in the footnotes section.

Using explanations in brackets after the term is a particularly good way of explaining abbreviations and acronyms. These tend to pass into common usage in the organisation without anyone remembering after a time what they originally stood for. At least the quality management manual will provide the real meaning for future generations of staff to know.

## *Be consistent*

◆ **Elegant variation**
The *fee* must be arranged before the work is begun. When the *price* has been agreed the account manager must be informed of the *cost*. If the account manager agrees to the *charge*, they should sign Form 2 to confirm the *expense*. *Reader's question:* are fee, price, cost, charge and expense all the same?

When you were taught to write essays at school, you were probably encouraged to use alternative words throughout a text to express the same idea, to avoid dullness and repetition. This technique is known as elegant variation.

However, elegant variation is out of place in the quality management manual. If you refer to the same thing in different ways, the reader will be puzzled and spend time wondering if you are talking about the same thing or something different.

It is very easy to use variations without intending to. It might be a good idea to create a working glossary for yourself as you write, so that you can consciously decide how best to refer to things and keep to it.

### *Use true verbs, not noun-verbs*

Instead of using a simple verb (like 'confirm') some people will turn it into a noun ('confirmation') which they then use with a more general verb like 'make' or 'do'. So the one word 'confirm' becomes three words 'make a confirmation'. This gives the reader more work to do and obscures the meaning without adding to the sense of what you are trying to say.

◆

| Verb + noun | Verb |
|---|---|
| carry out a fitting | fit |
| give notification | notify |
| make a confirmation | confirm |
| make an entry | enter |
| make a reservation | reserve |
| reach a conclusion | conclude |

### *Use personal pronouns*

Official documents are increasingly moving away from impersonal styles, where people are referred to by impersonal titles, to personal styles, which make explicit the fact that the document is communicating directly with the reader as an individual. This change makes writing flow much more easily and clarifies the relevance of the text to the reader.

You may be uncomfortable with this style because it seems rather informal, but remember that the importance of the information or instructions you are giving is not going to be affected by a more personal style: it will just be that much clearer and more effective.

◆ **Impersonal style**
The supplier should complete and return the form to the company as soon as possible. The buying department will phone the supplier if the quote is successful.

◆ **Personal style**
You should complete and return the form to us as soon as possible. They will phone you if your quote has been successful.

# Rules for sentences

These rules move on from using words to look at how clear sentences should be put together.

### *Use short sentences*

This is one of the first rules of writing informational material. In the previous section of this chapter we talked about how using a lot of words can obscure sense. In addition, long sentences usually contain a number of points for the reader to absorb all at once. Whereas full stops give the reader time to pause and internalise each point before moving on, single sentences don't. Several points in one sentence can therefore be quite confusing.

◆

**Procedures – the wrong way**
5.1.11
The alarm list highlights any non-standard prices that are applicable to orders. Non-standard price orders are checked using the customer discount book.

**Procedures – the right way**

5.1.11
Check the orders to see if any of them are for items at non-standard prices. You will find information about non-standard prices on the alarm list.

5.1.12
If you find any non-standard price orders, check them against the customer discount book to find out what price you should charge.

So the rule is: keep to one main point per sentence and keep it short. A rule of thumb for length is about 25 words.

Experience has shown that the one main point per sentence rule can also usefully be adapted to the one main point per procedure rule. There may be more than one sentence in each procedure, but they should all be closely related to a single main point.

This is often a difficult discipline to follow. You will find as you write the procedures that extra details crop up, and that the easiest way to deal with them is to slip them in almost as asides to the procedure you are working on. The other option you have, to add more procedures, may seem unattractive because increasing the number of procedures will make the activity you are defining seem even more complicated.

But it is well worth persevering with this rule. It is powerful because it relates directly to how you are thinking through and structuring what you are saying. Checking for one main point per sentence or procedure will help you check that your explanations and procedures are clearly and logically thought out.

## Use lists

◆ **Lists**
When you receive a delivery:
1. Record all the item numbers on the Goods Received form.
2. Check this against the invoice to see that all the items ordered have been sent.
3. Give the completed Goods Received form to your supervisor.

Lists are another way of breaking up information into manageable pieces for the reader to absorb. You can spot the opportunity for a list when you notice lots of *ands* in your text, or lots of commas, or repetition of the word *or*, or the words *first, second and third*, or repetition of the conjunction *when*. A list allows you to set out a lot of information relating to a common point in a way which is easy for the reader to absorb, and particularly easy to refer to.

Lists of points which are sequential – these are most likely to be instructions – should be numbered. Otherwise, signal the items in a list by using bullets or dashes.

You will find more guidance about setting out lists in Chapter 8, *Designing the Quality Management Manual*.

## Use parallel structures

◆ **Parallel structures in lists**
The warehouse manager must:
– calculate the total hours that have been worked
– enter any overtime in red pen.

Remember that if you are writing similar kinds of information a number of times, you should use the same types of words and sentence structures each time. The reader will recognise the pattern which you have established and associate similar pieces of information quite naturally. This is particularly necessary when you are using lists. Each element of the list needs to be parallel grammatically with all the others.

## Use active sentence constructions

This rule is probably the second most important rule of clear informational writing. It is to do with how you approach your sentences, with the types of sentence structures you choose to convey information and instructions.

As with the rule about short sentences, this is a powerful rule because it affects the way you think through what you need to say.

In explaining the theory behind active and passive sentence constructions, mysterious grammatical terms and concepts will occur. If the explanation doesn't mean anything to you, don't worry: the examples should make the point!

In a normal active sentence construction there are 3 elements: subject, verb and object. Using this kind of simple sentence structure consistently will not win you the Nobel Prize for literature, but it will help to minimise the interpretative demands you are making on your readers, who need to know exactly what this sentence structure is designed to tell them:

1.  Who has to do the task.

2.  What action the task requires.

3.  Who or what the action affects.

You may by now have every intention of using only short, simple sentences. But be prepared for what will happen when you start to write! The phenomenon known as the passive is waiting in the wings.

Passive sentence constructions are made up of the same three elements, subject, verb and object. The difference is in the ordering of the elements and what that implies.

This change in the order of the elements in the sentence is actually significant because:

* it makes the reader spend time working out who is doing what to whom. There is considerable evidence that people turn passive constructions back to active constructions in their heads, so that they can understand them

* it creates a writing style which is heavy and relatively difficult to understand – a style with all the connotations of the word 'passive', in fact

* more importantly, it allows the writer to evade the question of who is doing the action. This is because sentences will work without stated objects. They won't work without subjects.

◆ **Elements of a sentence**
*The sales clerk*
1.  The person the sentence is about – the subject
*opens*
2.  The action that takes place – the verb
*the letters*
3.  The thing that the action is done to – the object.

◆ **Passive sentences**
*The letters*
1.  The thing the action is done to – the subject
*are opened*
2.  The action – the verb
*by the sales clerk.*
3.  The person who does the action – the object

So as you start to write the procedures, you are likely to find it seductively easy to slip into the passive voice, where things are reviewed, approved, documented and assessed, without anyone in particular being responsible.

Of course, passive sentences have their place, particularly if the thing to be done is more important than who does it or if you don't know who or what might do it.

But for informational writing, learn to recognise the passive voice and keep its use to a minimum. Over-use of passive constructions is a besetting sin of this kind of text, helping to make it heavy, irritatingly difficult to work out and often still unclear when you've sorted out how the sentence works.

In the example below, we have changed the procedure by using an active sentence structure. Notice how other changes have had to be made to the text, in keeping with the more direct and personal tone associated with active verbs.

**Passive**
3.1.1 When requested by the customer, Belsize Manufacturing Ltd will produce a quotation. The quotation must contain as a minimum:
a   A unique reference
b   The customer name and address
c   The quantity and description of the goods to be supplied
d   The price
e   The delivery period, where different to that quoted on the Price List
f   Terms and conditions of the order.
When enquiries are received through Trade Advertising Enquiry forms, then these will be passed to official agents for progressing. Copies of these forms will be taken for subsequent review.

**Active**
3.1.1 When the customer requests it, you should provide a quotation. This quotation must contain as a minimum:
a   A unique reference
b   The customer name and address
c   The quantity and description of the goods to be supplied
d   The price
e   The delivery period, where it is different to that quoted on the Price List
f   Terms and conditions of the order.
3.1.2 When you receive an order through the Trade Advertising Enquiry forms, pass it on to the company's official agents for them to follow up. Remember to take copies of these Enquiry forms, so that you can review the results of each enquiry later (see Procedure 6.2).

## Write positively

And finally, write positively. Research has shown that people absorb information significantly better if it is expressed positively rather than negatively – even though the meaning is virtually the same. This is because a negative word or sentence will tell you what not to do, but leaves you to work out what you should do for yourself.

And of course, avoid double negatives at all costs: sometimes they are quite safe, but on other occasions no one can work out what they mean.

◆
**Negative**
Unstamped parcels must not be sent out.
**Positive**
Stamp all parcels before sending them out.
**Negative**
Don't leave tanks unfilled at the of end of the day.
**Positive**
Fill up all the tanks at the end the day.

# Editing your work

In the world of writing, nobody ever gets it right first time. You should allow plenty of time to edit and refine the style of your work. You will probably find that as you edit you will make significant changes to vocabulary and length: the finished work is likely to be shorter and simpler.

As you edit, keep your audience in mind and read what you have written from their perspective. Of course, it is difficult to be objective about your own work. You will always be hampered by the fact that you know what you meant when you wrote it.

For this reason, it is a good idea to test your drafts on an actual user before you finalise the text. This will give you reliable feedback about whether what you have said is clear or not. Don't worry if feedback is negative at times: you didn't expect to get it right first time, after all.

## *Case Study*

### *Ropers and the Receivers – Matching Practice and Procedures*

It was a big surprise to everyone, including members of the Ropers board themselves, when on 8 October 1992 the company's cash resources ran out and the company went into official liquidation.

Ropers was a niche market supplier of high-quality, complex electronic switching devices. These were used primarily in defence equipment, the Ministry of Defence being Ropers' main customer. In spite of the recent reductions in arms procurement, orders for the Ropers product had remained steady, and the board was confident that their efforts to find new export markets would pay off.

Monthly management accounts showed that costs had not risen significantly over the previous three years. One advantage of the recession was that materials and wage costs had stopped rising.

Yet in spite of this apparently satisfactory situation, the fact remained that by October 1992 the company had nearly run out of money, and was unable to fund the production it needed to fulfil its order book.

This was the situation when the company's accountants Lewis and Bland were called in on that October day. The man in charge of the Ropers account was an American called Ralph Donaldson. Donaldson had plenty of experience in recent months of going into established British companies and uncovering the same sorry story: falls in order books, over-exposure to the banks and their rising interest rates, and ageing management boards unable to find aggressive new strategies to combat the recession. Donaldson knew what he was looking for and although he did not relish the assignment, he was not anticipating any problems in establishing the causes of Ropers' problems.

By 10 October, however, he was completely puzzled. He had made all his usual checks and found nothing significantly wrong with the company. Orders were steady and expenses running at an even rate, well below break-even at the current selling price of the switches. Bank lendings had been small, until the last three months when the company had suddenly shot to its overdraft limit.

Donaldson decided to take a look at the pattern of debtor days to see if the MoD had taken longer than its customary 60 days to pay its accounts over the last few months. He didn't think that the MoD would do this, or that Ropers' problems could be caused solely by such a change, but he was running out of ideas.

He looked at the computer print-out of debtor records over the last six months. Starting with the earliest record, he began to trace the progress of individual invoices and calculate debtor days for each one. After he had checked the first three months of his pile of records, he had seen nothing but a healthy pattern of debtor payments, all within 60 days. The only exceptions were with contracts where the amount was queried by one side or the other. Donaldson sighed and rubbed his forehead wearily. He did not feel any closer to finding the solution and time was running out. Managers, shareholders and the workforce were all waiting impatiently for the results of his analysis to find out what had gone wrong.

Donaldson flipped over the sheets in front of him to the next page. He was now entering the period when the company's problems had really begun. He glanced at the page and then irritably flipped on to the next one and the one after that. For the last three months, invoicing had suddenly dropped dramatically. Donaldson immediately assumed he had been given the wrong sheets.

'How careless,' he fumed to himself. He would have to go back down to the computer room and get a fresh copy of the records, this time with all the data correct. He was halfway down the corridor before the truth struck him. It was so obvious it was unbelievable. It explained everything. Ropers had come to grief quite simply because for some reason something had gone wrong with the invoicing system.

Donaldson called an emergency board meeting and explained what he had found. A stunned silence greeted his disclosure. Then various members of the board began to object. How could such a stupid thing have happened? Donaldson was saying they did not know the elementary rules of business, even though they had been trading successfully for 50 years. But gradually the objections died down and the chairman took control. Turning to the others, he said,

'Something happened three months ago which must have led to this. Surely if we all think hard about it now we can come up with the answer. There's no point in trying to protect our backs at this stage: if we don't come up with a good answer fast, we're all out of business.'

Then one of the board members, David Jarrell, who was the executive sponsor for the quality management system the company was introducing, asked to speak. He pointed out quietly that the problem coincided exactly with the introduction of new procedures, as defined in the latest version of the company's quality procedures manual. He promised to lead a full investigation and to report to the board in the next few days. In the meantime, Donaldson could concentrate his energies on persuading the banks to renew their support for Ropers, until the backlog of invoices could be processed and the cash could start flowing again.

David Jarrell went straight to the accounts department and called all the staff together. Once they knew what they were looking for, the staff did not take long to find the root of the trouble. It lay, as Jarrell had immediately suspected, in the new quality management manual.

The manual was a very solid, weighty document – literally. It had been prepared by a team of engineers over the past year. The engineers had conducted interviews with all the departments in the company and then compiled the procedures. They had then handed back the procedures to the departments for checking.

In the discussions now taking place in the accounts department, it emerged that no one had really checked through the document properly. It was just too long, too detailed and too difficult to check.

Mrs Fields, head of accounts, admitted that she had not scrutinised the manual as closely as she should have.

'But,' she pointed out, 'this is – well was – one of the few departments that was working like clockwork. I felt I didn't need to get all involved in these new procedures. There was nothing we had to change, really. I understood we could go on just as we always had. And the team writing the manual didn't seem too worried. They said they didn't understand our bit of it anyway. and it was up to us to carry on.'

In fact the new procedures had a fatal flaw. They did cover invoicing procedures, in fact there were 15 pages of them. But they were concerned with how to process invoices within the department. They didn't deal with the rather critical point of who should be raising the invoices in the first place and how often.

After the meeting, Jarrell stared at the invoicing section of the manual for about half an hour. What it said was:

> 10.6  Accounts on their falling due for dispatch to the customer should be actioned in accordance with company regulations. Upon completion of the pre-invoice procedure Accounts should receive the following having been produced by the computer system:
> - a green copy delivery note
> - a white copy annotated with the order number.
> The pre-invoice is despatched to the customer.

The procedure was confusing to Jarrell in many ways, but he reserved his analysis for the sentence 'Accounts should receive the following...'. The team who had written the manual had intended this to mean that the computer would provide the documentation to the department, which would then send out the pre-invoice form to the customer. But who was to tell the computer? There seemed to be a missing link.

More investigation provided Jarrell with the answer he had been looking for. Some invoicing had been carried out: when a project was completely finished. At this point the procedures required the project managers to fill in a project completion form and send it to accounts. But this wasn't enough to sustain the company's cashflow. Some orders took months to complete.

In the past, there had been a system of stage invoicing. It had been quite informally done. Project managers would agree stage payments with the clients and then jot down what had been decided on a piece of paper which they would pass to Mrs Fields.

When the new procedures came in and Mrs Fields stopped receiving pieces of paper, she naturally assumed that proper invoices were being raised instead, going through the system. When the project managers saw that there was no mention of stage invoicing in their procedures, they naturally assumed that Mrs Fields had taken responsibility for arranging this herself directly with the clients. The project managers had every reason to believe that this was so, since they had made the point very strongly to the quality management team that they didn't think they should be responsible for negotiating financial details with the client. This was, in their view, the job of the accounts department. And since the quality management team had listened sympathetically, they assumed the change had taken place.

And in any case none of the project managers had actually read the procedures for the accounts department, or vice versa. Both sides assumed that there would be nothing of relevance to them in other people's procedures. The manual contained no kind of overview diagram or description to show how departments related to each other, or how they shared the same clients.

On 15 October, exactly a week after the crisis had been announced, David Jarrell reported to the board. He explained what had happened and proposed that the manual should be withdrawn immediately. It would have to be re-thought and restructured so that everyone could see much more clearly what procedures were being proposed and who was to be responsible for them. The board accepted his proposal and the company survived to tell the tale of how its quality management manual brought it to the verge of bankruptcy.

# Designing the Quality Management Manual 8

## The importance of good design

The most obvious function of good design is to make the quality manual more attractive. But good design isn't just something superficial: it's something which will make the content of the manual clearer, more accessible and more usable. We all know how frustrating it is to try to find out something we need to know from badly designed information – perhaps how to pay a bill, or order something by post. The information we need is there somewhere, but it isn't organised and designed in the way we expect or need it to be. If the quality manual is not clearly set out, your users will experience just that frustration. They will find themselves leafing through it, trying to remember where they thought they saw a particular piece of information, without any systematic way of approaching the text to find out what they want. On the other hand, a well-designed manual will positively invite people to use it, because it will help them to solve their problems rather than causing them more. Good graphic design does this by making the structure of the information clear at every opportunity.

## Good design – buy it in or develop your own?

This chapter aims to give you enough guidance to design your own manual. It introduces the basic concepts and techniques behind good design. Effective design takes time, and you should expect to take some time to try different ideas and combinations until you are happy with the result. No professional designer would expect to come up with the right solution straight away, and neither should you.

If your organisation has invested in DTP (desktop publishing) equipment you will obviously want to use it to achieve a more professional-looking result. However, you should beware of the 'look, ma, no hands' syndrome – showing off all the automated features of your DTP system such as shadow boxes, numerous fonts and tinted backgrounds. Effective design is usually very simple – its goal is to show the structure of the information, not to distract readers with special effects.

Word processing software often comes with pre-designed 'templates' for common business documents – some of these are very good, others less so. This chapter should help you decide.

If you do not have the time or skills in-house, you can get professional information design consultants to format the manual for you, or to develop a style for you to implement yourself. All you have to do then is to key in text, apply preset styles and arrange to have the manual printed out and duplicated. If you decide to use professionals, this chapter will help you to know what to look for in a good design, and act as a starting point for discussions with your supplier.

Design can make your manual work better for its users in three main ways:

- it makes the content of the manual more accessible – helping users to *find* the information

- it makes the manual legible – helping users to *read* the information

- it can make the meaning of the text clearer – helping users to *understand* the information.

### Formats and bindings that make the text accessible

The binding method you choose will have an impact on how easy it is to use the manual. The first requirement is that the binder should open flat without springing shut – this rules out most thermoplastic glue binding and the sort of binders that uses plastic strips to clamp the pages of the document together at one edge.

The most common method is the ring-binder. They are easy to buy and use and are available in a wide range of capacities and sizes. Documents can also easily be updated with amended pages, and pages can be removed for photocopying (useful if you are including forms and other working tools in the manual). However, some organisations prefer not to issue individual update sheets but to reprint and issue a whole new edition when major changes have to be made. If that is the case, you can use more permanent forms of binding. Plastic comb or wire binding is convenient and effective – in-house reprographics departments and high street instant print shops usually offer it, or you can buy equipment from office supplies companies.

Most quality manuals are in the standard A4 format (210mm × 297mm). Some companies issue manuals or parts of manuals in other formats – for example, in personal organiser format – so that employees can carry relevant sections along with their diaries.

How many binders should you use? Because the quality policy manual is normally a relatively short document it is common to bind it in with the quality procedures manual. However, this means that the procedures manual – the document you want employees to use to structure their work – is less accessible than the policy manual, which they will rarely need to refer to. For this reason, we suggest always binding them separately, even if the policy manual is quite short.

## Access features

A well-designed document will help people to find the information they need quickly and easily. Think about how people are going to use it – few will read it through from beginning to end. Instead, the manual will mostly be used to look up a particular fact or procedure. If people find it hard to do this your quality system will not work as well as it should, even though all the right procedures are outlined in the manual.

◆ Access features are such things as:
– covers
– contents lists
– section starts
– headings
– running heads
– page numbers
– indexes

There are a number of access features you can use to help your readers. If you use them all carefully, they will make a very significant contribution to the usability of your manual.

### Covers

The cover should identify the manual for what it is and give the user an immediate overview of its contents. The easiest way to do this is to include major section titles under the main title (see Figure 31).

As with all aspects of design, remember the user's needs. If your manual is in several volumes, for example, it doesn't help if they all look alike, differentiated only by information in small type. Keep the design of the cover simple, so that the user can comfortably absorb the information on it.

If your manual is bound in a ring-binder, you can get binders with full-size clear pockets on the front to take a printed sheet. If you are comb or wire binding, then consider using a clear acetate sheet at the front rather than card covers with a small window – this will give you a full page to display information to the best effect, rather than a few square centimetres.

**The Quality Policy Manual**
for Company A Ltd

1 Quality policy statement
2 Company structure
3 ISO9000 conformance table

**Figure 31** *The cover*

### *Title page*

If your manual is comb or wire bound, and you have followed the guidelines above on the cover, you won't need a title page – the cover has the same function. But if you are using a ring-binder, you should also have a title page with the same information on it as the cover.

### *Contents lists*

The contents list should list all the headings you have used in the document, with page numbers. The design of the contents list can help users to see the structure of the manual and thus to find their way around it. So use a clear hierarchy of headings, with extra space between major sections (see Figure 32).

Assembling the contents page may actually be your first chance to see the headings you have used all in one place. Make sure they work well as a set, as they must:

- provide a complete overview of the contents of the document for new users
- act as an index for experienced users.

If the headings don't work well together, you should rewrite them so that they seem logical and connected. By reading them, your readers should be able to get an overview of the content and identify the section that is most likely to be relevant to their query.

Because the contents list summarises the contents of a manual, it should come first so that it is easy to find. It is less effective if the reader has to wade through a succession of amendment registers, circulation lists and prefaces to find it.

In order to comply with ISO9000, some sections of your manual may have a heading but no real content, beyond a statement that the company does not need a policy on, say, testing equipment. It is helpful to readers if these sections could be marked in the contents list, perhaps with an asterisk linked to a footnote.

Your instinct may well be to range page numbers to the right, so that they look neat. However, if you think about how you use the contents list you will realise that you always read the number straight after the text describing the particular section of the manual. So it makes sense to put the number straight after the text, so that your eye doesn't have to jump across a space to find it. It is actually quite difficult to relate a number to a line of text across a large gap.

### Contents

**1   Quality policy statement  5**
1.1  Statement  6
1.2  Signature of the chief executive  7

**2   Structure of company A  8**
2.1  Diagram of organisational structure  8
2.2  Description of roles  9
2.3  Quality management system  12

**3   ISO9000 requirements  22**
3.1  Table of requirements referenced to
       company A procedures  53

**Figure 32** *Contents list*

## Section starts

New sections need clear starting points – probably a new page for each start, and graphic signalling using any devices available to make the sections stand out. Rules, boxes and extra large type will help you to give prominence to section starts: don't be afraid to be bold (see Figure 33).

**3** Operations
    Management

**Figure 33** *Section starts*

If most of the sections in your manual are long, you can use tabbed index pages to help people go straight to the section they need.

### Headings

Headings are the most obvious access device. When we discussed contents lists we referred to the importance of headings working together as a set. You should also consider how the heading relates to the text that follows. It is common to see headings that mean nothing until you have read the text. But if they are to act as access devices, it is best if headings include a short translation of technical terms, or voice questions that the reader might have before they have read the text.

For example, we wrote 'Widows and orphans' as a heading for a section later on in this chapter. It is actually printers' jargon for the single words or lines that can become isolated at the foot or top of pages, so we rewrote the heading as 'Controlling page breaks: widows and orphans'.

### Running heads

Running heads can be at the top or bottom of the page – word processing programs usually call them 'headers' and 'footers'. They are used to carry over section headings from one page to the next, so that users can orientate themselves quickly when they flick though the manual.

Running heads, like headings in the text, should be arranged hierarchically. It should be possible to see as you flick through the pages what major section you are in, and which subsection is on each page. However, don't go too far up the hierarchy in the running heads. It is not necessary to make the title of the manual itself the most prominent item. From the user's point of view it isn't very important – after all, they know what manual they are holding. So set the main title quite small where it won't get in the way, and give greater priority to information that helps the reader to navigate around the manual. This also applies to version control information; this is information that helps you keep track of different versions of the manual – it normally includes the issue date, a version number, and perhaps the name of the computer file where it can be found.

### Page numbers

Page numbers are the most basic way of making a document accessible: make sure you include them and that they are clear and in the right place – either centred or on the outside of the page. To make updating easy, you can start a new series of page numbers for each major section in your manual. Section 3 would have pages numbered 3.1, 3.2, and so on.

## *Indexes*

Indexes are the only way that you can set about finding specific topics in a document, without having to guess what section they might be in. However, they are also difficult and time-consuming to compile properly. Someone has to go through every page of your document and make a judgement about what items in the page are key items which users are likely to want to find. These items are then listed alphabetically with page references. The better word processors have indexing features that automate the page referencing – you 'tag' words or phrases that you want to appear in the index and the program compiles a list of them, together with page references.

◆ **Index entry**
*policy*, quality of in the organisation

If you have used plenty of informative headings, an easier way to make up an index is to list them in alphabetical order, using the contents list as your starting point. You will probably have to rephrase the headings so that you can alphabetise the key points. They will sound rather odd, but they will be useful to the user.

# Design techniques: making information legible

Legibility is about making sure that your readers can see the text clearly. Poorly legibility slows readers down and increases the risk of them making mistakes – not spotting information they are searching for, or misreading words. And they are less likely to persevere with difficult information.

It's important not to judge legibility from your computer screen. The type may look larger or smaller on screen than it will when printed, so print out samples before you settle on an appropriate style.

For text to be legible, a number of different factors have to work together. There is a close interrelationship between:

- typeface

- type size

- line length

- line spacing.

### Typeface

Laser printers are now affordable by most businesses, and most come with a reasonable range of fonts. You will almost certainly have Times Roman (a typeface with 'serifs' – the small strokes you see at the ends of letters) and Helvetica (a typeface without serifs, known as a 'sans serif'). They might be called Dutch and Swiss, depending on your system. These have become the workhorse typefaces of business documents, although you may well have a number of other fonts available.

For continuous text, serif typefaces are generally considered most legible. Times would be a safe choice as your main typeface. You can then use Helvetica for headings and tables – it is particularly clear, and the change of typeface will add to the distinctiveness of the headings.

### Type size

◆ **Examples of type sizes**

9 pt: This is probably the smallest type size for continuous text

11 pt: This is probably the largest type size for continuous text

9 pt Times: This looks smaller than Helvetica

9 pt Helvetica: This looks larger than Times

Type is measured in points. In DTP systems there are 72 points to an inch. Within reason, the size of type is not often a problem for legibility. As a general guide, the smallest size of type you should use for continuous reading matter is 9 pt, and the largest 11 pt. These are roughly equivalent to 12 pitch and 10 pitch typewriter faces. For headings, you may want to use 12 or 14 pt type, with 18 or 20 pt for major section titles.

The point size of type is measured from the top of the ascender (ie, the highest point in a 'k') to the bottom of the descender (the lowest point on a 'p'). So because the proportion of the x-height (the bit in the middle) is different in each typeface, the actual appearing size of the type can be different too. In practical terms, this means that you have to allow for the fact that Helvetica will always look significantly bigger than Times in the same point size.

### Line length

Line length is defined by the number of words per sentence. Relatively short lines make information much easier to follow than longer ones – the reader can get physically as well as mentally lost. On the other hand, lines which are too short create too many line breaks, making it difficult for the reader to make sense of the information.

The line length that is generally recommended is 8–12 words per line, or 50–70 characters. On an A4 page this means leaving generous margins. You may feel this is a waste of paper, but do not be tempted to cram the page with words – you will greatly reduce the chances of your manual being read. In the long run this is a far greater waste of your resources.

---

*Example of line lengths*
It is our policy to provide installation and maintenance services on our customers' computer equipment to optimise performance. The range of services includes the provision of new equipment installation services, scheduled maintenance and unscheduled maintenance against call-out.

---

All word processors allow you to justify the lines – to add extra space between words in order to achieve a straight right-hand edge. This does not help legibility, although it can give your document a more formal appearance. Many professional designers prefer not to justify type, as the uneven word spacing gives a patchy appearance to the column of type. For narrow columns, such as marginal notes or table captions, you should switch justification off.

## Line spacing (leading)

Line spacing is also called 'leading', reflecting the old practice of spacing metal type with thin strips of lead. The right leading is probably the most important tool for achieving good legibility – even if your type is not as legible as it might be, adding extra space between the lines can make it easier for the eye to follow them. The leading should be set to at least 120–130 per cent of the type size – so 10 pt Times should be given at least 12 pt leading, and will be even clearer with 14 pt leading.

## Capitals and small letters

It is tempting in a formal document like the procedures manual, for example, to use capital letters in two ways:

- at the start of words, to give emphasis or importance to particular terms
- for whole words and sentences, for emphasis.

But capitals letters are actually difficult to read. They work well at the start of sentences because they cause a visual break in the text, but they will have the same effect in the middle of a sentence: that is, they will cause the reader to pause.

Whole words written in capital letters are also difficult to read. Because capitals do not have descenders, words printed in small

◆ *Compare*
3.4.5 When a copy of the Delivery Note is returned from the warehouse for your records, file it by Order Number in the Delivery Note File.
*with*
3.4.5 When a copy of the delivery note is returned from the warehouse for your records, file it by order number in the delivery note file.

letters have a much more distinctive word shape than words printed in capitals only. Capitals are acceptable for short headings, but not for continuous text.

## Design techniques for organising information

Graphic design can help to make your meaning much clearer by highlighting and defining the underlying structure of what you are saying.

We have already discussed the importance of clear hierarchies of headings. There are also principles for laying out pages and for design.

### Headings

◆ **Distinctions between levels of headings**

**A Head**

**B head**

C head

C head

C head

**B head**

**A Head**

Headings help users to find their way around individual pages. They need to stand out from the main text and at the same time relate clearly to the text they belong to. However, the most important thing about the design of headings is to make sure that you use clear typographic distinctions between headings of different levels. This makes the relationship between the sections of text clear, as well as making them easy to find. It is this ability to create clear distinctions between levels of text that makes DTP so useful.

Each heading needs to be prominent enough to make it clear that it is 'in force' until the next heading of the same status. In other words, it needs to dominate visually the lower levels of heading that follow it – in typography things that are bigger and darker are seen as more important than things that are smaller or lighter.

Space is important too, to signal the importance of headings. The more prominent headings should have more space above them (and they'll probably need some space below, too, so they don't crowd the following text). It is normal to force a new page start for the highest level headings.

It is important to be consistent and to be careful to use the right style of heading for the right level. If you don't, you will confuse the structure of the document rather than making it clearer.

◆ **Using lists**
Supplies of forms are kept:
– in the stock cupboard
– in the quality management office
– in the company library.

### Lists

We looked at when to use lists in Chapter 7, *Writing the Quality Management Manual*. The structure of lists can be emphasised by using dashes or bullet points before each item in the list. This graphic treatment makes the list easy to identify and remember.

# Design techniques for laying out pages

Good layout is about making sure that information lies sensibly on the page, that pieces of information which belong together in terms of their meaning are physically grouped together. Information which is visually lost gets conceptually lost as well.

Design is governed by a few simple rules that are based on our perceptual systems:

- things that look alike are seen as belonging to the same category. So, for example, all procedures should be laid out in the same way, so that they will be immediately recognisable.

- things that are close together are seen as related. So if you are starting something new, take care to use enough space to make it seem separate from what went before.

- things that are enclosed in the same space are seen as related. This is an important principle behind table design – lines between things, or boxes around them, use this principle.

## *Controlling page breaks: widows and orphans*

Page breaks need watching too. As you move from one page to another, it is easy to forget to check what is happening between the pages. The two most common problems are known as widows and orphans.

A widow is a single word which is left over from a paragraph to sit by itself at the top of a page.

An orphan is a heading (or the first line of a paragraph, but this is not a serious problem) which has become separated from the rest of the paragraph by a page break. It sits by itself at the bottom of the page. The solution to both of these problems is to force the page break to happen where you want it – in the case of the widow, you should force at least one more line over onto the new page with the widow. Likewise, you should force the page break just before the orphan.

Many word processors have an option called 'keep with next paragraph' which you can select for heading styles – this prevents them being orphaned. There may also be a general option called 'widow control' or something similar.

**◆ Examples of widows and orphans**

**Widow**

processing.
When a copy of the delivery note is returned from the warehouse for your records.

**Orphan**
3.1.4   If the item is out of stock, contact the customer personally by phone.
**A3.2   Classifying orders**

## *Using space*

Don't be afraid of using space if it makes the manual clearer. In the procedures manual, for example, you should start a new page for each section of the procedures, even if you still have most of a page left over at the end of the section before. If you have to transfer a whole paragraph to the next page to avoid a difficult page break, then do it. It may be good ecology to save paper by filling every page, but it's bad communication – and ultimately bad ecology if the information is unread and therefore wasted.

# Designing tables

The design techniques we have looked at so far have been about using text. But text is not the only way to present information. There are obvious places for tables throughout the quality manual. The conformance table at the end of the quality policy manual is an important example.

Tables will differ in size and complexity. The design approach we suggest here is easy to implement if you have a DTP system and is suitable for most tables. If you don't have a DTP system, you won't be able to do much with type, but you can use the rest of the suggestions given here. However, you may need to devise special treatments if these suggestions don't work with the material you have.

## Typeface

You will usually need to use a smaller type size for tables than for the main text and you can use a condensed font, if you have it available, where space is tight.

## Vertical and horizontal rules

You should make generous use of horizontal rules (lines) in tables. They help in reading across the table, and by varying the thickness you can emphasise different sections.

You will be able to set up tables with horizontal rules on the simplest word processors. On more sophisticated programs you will find a table design facility. This creates cells into which you can type information, and it can draw both horizontal and vertical rules of different thicknesses. However, vertical rules can usually be omitted – the information in the columns is well enough aligned to allow the space between the columns to do the same job. If many of the cells are left blank, vertical rules might be needed (see Figure 34).

## Column headings

Column headings should be short (abbreviate if you have to). If the main content of the table is text, rather than numbers, make sure the column headings look distinctive – use italic, for example. If the table is longer than a single page, repeat the column headings on the second page.

## Row headings

Row headings should also be as short as possible. If they go onto a second line, make sure this isn't mistaken for a new heading – indent the turnover line, or use horizontal rules between rows.

## Laying out tables

The widths of the columns will vary with their content and headings. Set one tab setting for each column so that you can adjust the tabs when all the content has been entered. When you have finished, the columns of your table should look equally spaced.

**Written customer complaints to Head Office**

|  | 1991 | 1992 |
|---|---|---|
| Faulty goods | 203 | 19 |
| Warranty returns | 92 | 17 |
| Service complaints | 78 | 1 |
| Other | 14 | 4 |
| Total | 287 | 41 |

**Figure 34** *Tables*

# Diagrams

We have already suggested quite a variety of ways of creating and using diagrams in the quality manual:

- organisation charts
- management process diagrams
- procedures diagrams
- data flow diagrams.

Here we look at the principles underlying effective diagrams, so that you can go on to develop your own diagrams as you need them.

*Writing and designing*

Good diagrams are logical and consistent. And the secret of achieving logical, consistent diagrams is to analyse the elements which make up the diagram before you start, and to decide on ways of treating these elements that will be common for all the diagrams you create. This was the principle behind the data flow diagram methodology we looked at in Chapter 6, *Workplace References*.

Some elements of typical diagrams (see Figure 35) will be:

- the organisation: by convention in quality management, a triangle

- things: people, procedures, roles

- relationships: linked sequentially through time, linked by theme, permanently linked, linked from time to time.

- directions: towards, away from, through

- levels: steps, parallel lines.

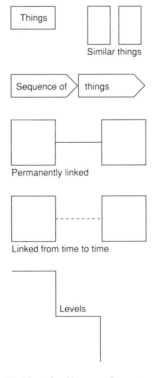

**Figure 35** *Ideas for diagram elements*

Experiment with arranging the elements of your diagram in different ways for the best result. Think about whether the diagram looks horizontal or vertical, portrait or landscape. When you think you've got it right, ask people what they think the diagram means. The results can be quite surprising.

A word of warning: keep diagrams simple. If you have a computer to hand, you may be tempted to experiment with drawing software and start introducing novelty features. But these things can easily get in the way of what you are trying to show – we have all had the experience of peering at computer graphics in our local newsletters and saying, 'but what exactly *is* it?' The basic tools of any drawing software are enough to allow you to diagram neatly and effectively.

◆ Say no to:
– 3-D lettering
– clipart
– exotic tints and textures

Keep to:
– basic tint patterns
– shadow boxes
– boxes, rules and arrows.

# Planning the design

Planning a design means:

- identifying all the elements which will have to be designed

- thinking about how to treat these elements individually

- thinking about how the design for all the elements will work as a set.

◆ Elements for design will be things like:
– headings – at least 4
– tables of contents
– normal text
– lists
– running heads
– numbering systems
– captions to diagrams
– page numbers.

## *Identifying elements*

By the time you come to think about the design of the quality manual, you will have a pretty good idea of what the content and structure of the information in it is going to be. You now need to make detailed decisions about how the final version will be organised – you can do this by marking up a draft copy. You can then analyse the elements which will need a design style.

## *How to treat different elements*

When you look at these elements individually, consider:

- the technical options you have for creating your design

- any legibility or readability constraints which apply.

The design principles given earlier in this chapter are a good place to start for basic decisions about type size, heading styles, and so on.

*Writing and designing*

### *Putting the design together*

◆ Some of the
problems you may
encounter are:
– headings too similar
  in size
– odd combinations of
  typefaces
– too little space
  (leading)
– rules which are too
  weak or too heavy
– tints which are too
  heavy or too light.

It is at this point that your creative judgement, as well as your common sense, comes into play. Try out combinations of the styles you have chosen and spot the problems. Don't be tempted to close your eyes to problems at this stage, thinking it won't matter. People have an uncanny sensitivity to design weaknesses. For example, if heading levels look too similar, people will confuse them; if dividing rules are too weak, they will miss them. Keep trying until you are convinced that your design is clear, robust and working well.

# Case Study

## XYZ Insulations Ltd – Making the Manual Usable

XYZ Insulations Limited regarded the rising tide of interest in ISO9000 in the UK in the late 1980s with a comfortable sense of superiority. They had been registered for years.

The company had grown steadily from its post-war beginnings by offering a basic range of insulation work to heating and ventilation contractors. As it grew, it attracted bigger and bigger clients, until in the 1970s it succeeded in securing its first government contract.

The question of quality control and registration was raised at that point by the inspectors from government procurement who vetted new suppliers. The board of XYZ agreed to think about adopting a quality management standard. They understood that it would help their business prospects with government procurement officers.

Then, as the 1970s drew to a close, XYZ discovered a whole new market. The asbestos scare was at its height and the government issued orders to remove all asbestos insulation from all its power stations throughout the country. This work required specialist skills which XYZ already had in place. Business boomed and profits rocketed. Stripping asbestos from miles of piping and cooling towers was a specialist, high-risk and high-priority service for which the government was prepared to pay a high price. Turnover grew to £8 million, with around 60 full-time employees.

It was during this period that XYZ achieved ISO9000 registration. The sensitive and high-risk nature of the asbestos-stripping work meant that the government procurers were more anxious than ever to have solid evidence of XYZ's competence for the task. At the same time, XYZ welcomed the opportunity to make sure for their own sake that proper procedures were followed throughout the company, safeguarding health and maintaining a high standard of work.

But as the 1980s drew to a close, the question that had been in the background during the boom years began inexorably to move to the foreground. The question was: What happens when the asbestos has all gone? By this stage operations at XYZ were totally dedicated to their lucrative market niche.

This decision point coincided with another. The founder and owner of the company was due to retire in 1991. Management faced the choice of accepting the rapid demise of XYZ when the asbestos had all gone, a demise sealed by the retirement of the owner. Alternatively management could use the next two years to effect a transition from its asbestos specialism and move back to the mainstream insulation market, under the aegis of a new chief executive. XYZ took the decision to survive.

The new company structure which was hammered out over the next weeks and months reflected the trend at the end of the 1980s as the boom years passed into recession. The plan was to make the company lean and flexible, able to respond to market opportunities quickly. Decision making was moved down from the top to newly created business units, which had to develop their own processes using the skills and experience of their staff.

XYZ spent heavily on management consultancy throughout the stages of planning and implementing this change management programme. The quality management standard proved its worth during this period by providing the consultants with a ready-made change management framework. They were able to work out for each of the new business units what its new management processes would be, and write up new procedures using a process which was familiar to the managers of the units from their experience of the standard.

But when the small business units received drafts of the new quality manual, the change management process suddenly hit a submerged rock. It quickly became clear that no one could use the new manuals. Although these manuals contained everything that staff needed to know to carry forward the changes they knew were essential, they weren't actually helping people to do this. Different personalities expressed their frustration in different ways: some simply ignored the manuals, hoping that somebody somewhere would soon explain what was going on, while others became annoyed and complained loud and long about how useless the manuals were. One sales manager, never noted for a sunny temper at the best of times, actually threw his copy across the room and bent the rings on the binder.

The consultancy team were soon made aware of this feedback. Staff were ready and willing to change procedures and processes, but they simply couldn't seem to make out what they were meant to do. Naturally the consultants were embarrassed about this, but they were also quite surprised. When they had undertaken the re-drafting work, they had been particularly careful to change the style and layout of the existing procedures as little as possible. In fact, they had been rather pleased with the sensitivity they had shown in producing new manuals which were so similar in style to the originals.

Some tactful questioning elicited some rather surprising results. In the past, although everyone had followed procedures they hadn't relied on the manual. The manual had been based largely on established practice. Any changes were quickly covered in training sessions, and the procedures passed on to newcomers by example and word of mouth, just as they always had been. The difference now was that the quality manuals represented significant changes in practice which couldn't just be explained in a training session or two: they actually needed to be used.

Because the problem was so urgent, the quality management consultants decided to call in information design expertise for a document appraisal study. The conclusions of this study showed that, although the quality manuals were quite clearly and logically written, they had been presented in a way which made far too many assumptions about their audience. They assumed, for example, that everyone would be familiar with the terminology of the ISO9000 standard and would know where to look for particular procedures. In fact this wasn't the case. Terms such as *contract review* or *process control* didn't actually mean much to staff. They needed to be able to see headings which related directly to the functions and departments with which they were familiar.

The manuals were re-drafted, re-structured, re-designed and re-issued. Initial responses were cautious. The new manuals looked better, but memories were still fresh of whole pages of procedures which had looked OK but which hadn't actually meant anything. Gradually, however, the tension eased. People could look at flowcharts and contents lists, running heads and margin notes, to find out where to look for information. And when they found it, it was easy to read and understand.

When the work of drafting the new manuals for the small business units was virtually completed, a representative from one of the business units raised an interesting point.

> Are we still all part of the same quality management system now? I know we all sort of follow the same rules, and we do things like accounts the same way, but we've got our own procedures now, and we'll be doing our audits separately. Doesn't that mean we really have our own quality systems?

This was an interesting question for the management consultants to consider. It reflected the discussions they had had early on with the XYZ board about the degree of centralisation versus decentralisation that was right for the new shape of the company. On the one hand, it was important for XYZ to retain some sense of corporate identity. On the other hand, it was also important for the new small business units to feel a real sense of independence and responsibility.

In the end, this issue was resolved in the case of the quality management system by the design of the manuals. The consultants suggested that XYZ should adopt an overall design style for the manuals that could be tailored through the use of colour and logos for each of the small business units. This design solution reflected the fact that, while the business units would share some policies and procedures, they would also have their own unique characteristics.

The business units themselves were very happy with this decision, as it helped them to feel a sense of their own identity, while at the same time linking them to each other and to the XYZ board.

# Part 4 Project Management

# Planning and Resourcing the Project 9

## Planning your resources

Writing the quality management manual is quite a considerable task, and in fact as we see in Chapter 11, *Assessment and After*, the work doesn't end with the first draft. The quality management manual will be part of a continuing cycle of audit and evaluation, resulting in corrections and changes which must then be monitored and controlled. So you need to think carefully about the resources that you have and the resources that you are going to need, both in the short and long term, to produce and maintain the manual and about where those resources will come from. If you under-resource the project, it will drift on slowly for months or even years. If you over-resource it, it may starve other parts of the organisation and take you away from your core business. It's no good having a first-class quality management manual if your delivery times have slipped because of it – the customer won't find that a very convincing excuse. You must balance priorities and resource the project to a level which is right for your budget and the time-scales you are working to.

▲ This chapter doesn't go into detail about setting up the quality management project. If you want to know more about project management, you should look up a book, such as *A practical guide to Project Management* by Celia Burton and Norma Michael (Kogan Page, 1992)

This chapter looks at the issues you will face in planning and resourcing the project in general terms. In Chapter 10, *Preparing the Quality Management Manual*, you will find more specific comments on how you might approach resourcing particular parts of the project.

## Using external consultants

Using external consultants is for most organisations the key resource issue to get right. Get it wrong, and the project becomes frustrating, expensive and probably unsuccessful. Get it right, and your internal input will be minimised and you will get where you want to go at a price you can afford to pay.

The obvious reasons why you might want to involve external quality management consultants in writing the quality management manual are:

◆ Research indicates that approximately 75 per cent of companies who are successful use external consultants. When you are considering the cost of consultancy, remember that you may be eligible for a DTI grant covering 50 per cent of quality management consultancy fees.

- you probably won't have the time in-house
- you probably won't have the expertise in-house.

Other reasons why you might want external consultants are:

- to carry weight with senior management, who won't be so inclined to ignore advice if they're paying for it
- to act as an external focus for resentment or upset which may occur as part of the change process.

The reasons to be careful about how you use external consultants for this task are:

- your budget. Consultancy doesn't come cheap. Justify it carefully.
- the quality of your quality management manual. You probably don't just want an off-the-shelf product. To suit your needs, the manual has to interpret the standard both in the language of accepted industry norms and your own internal culture, and that means working closely with the consultants.

There is a Goldilocks choice to be made about what level of external consultancy support will be right for you – two wrong options before you find the right one. The choices to avoid are:

- relying too much on consultancy
- not using enough consultancy.

### Too much consultancy

It is very tempting to parcel up the whole problem of the quality management manual and hand it on to someone else. You may not care about the cost, setting off a short-term cash outlay against the long-term cost of the disruption which would be caused by taking staff away from their responsibilities in your company.

Neat though it is, this formula won't work. The Franklin West case study at the end of this chapter is a sad but true account of what tends to happen if you hand over too much responsibility to outside consultants. You will end up with something which has been externally devised and which therefore doesn't have a place in your organisation at all – least of all at the heart of it, which is where the quality management manual needs to be.

You are probably using, or planning to use, too much consultancy, if:

- you have no plan for internal resource allocation to the project – you imagine it will just take a few days here and there

- you have no precise idea of what the consultants will be doing. When they start to tell you, you don't really understand what they're saying

- you don't exactly know what the consultants are doing when they come – you assume they're just getting on with it

- you don't even know exactly when the consultants are coming – you assume they're just getting on with it

- you don't really understand the sections of the manual as they are completed

- no one else in your company seems to understand the sections of the manual as they are completed either.

These scenarios are not exaggerations. There is a significant number of cases where, because of lack of understanding or lack of internal resources, the management of the project has been handed over more or less completely to external consultants, with generally poor results. You can't just buy your way into quality management – there has to be commitment as well.

### Not enough consultancy

At the other extreme, it is possible to be too independent and waste a lot of time getting the quality management manual completed and wrong. This can happen if, for example, you send a member of staff to a seminar where it all sounds very easy, or if you get yourself a copy of the ISO9000 quality management standard and decide that you can work it all out for yourself.

The truth is that ISO9000 is still something of a black art which has been developed over the years by professionals who know exactly what the standard means, what parts are flexible, what parts are not flexible, and how assessors think – all the tricks of the trade. Also ways of interpreting and applying the standard are evolving, in ways which it is difficult for the outsider to appreciate.

◆ An increasing number of industry sectors are interpreting the standard for their members. For example, the TickIT scheme presents the principles of ISO9000 in the language of the software industry. Check with your trade associations to see if there are any such developments within your own industry.

This situation is gradually changing, and it is now a good deal easier than it was even a few years ago to find out about what fulfilling the requirements of the quality management standard means. Indeed, this book is designed to go some way towards helping you to do just that.

But it is still unwise to go all the way to formal assessment without professional help, because you are quite simply reducing your chances of success. In most circumstances also it is not actually cost-effective to do everything yourself. Any cash savings will be offset by the expenditure of internal time, a lot of which can be wasted when you don't know quite what you are doing. Good specialists, like computer specialists, accountants and lawyers, should be cost-effective.

An example of a DIY quality management manual project that went wrong was brought to light recently when the company concerned failed registration and was referred to a quality management consultancy by the assessors, in this case the British Standards Institute. The manual in question was a substantial document reflecting a good deal of serious effort and logical thinking, but it did not separate out policy from procedures and workplace references, and consequently seemed muddled and impossible to assess to the BSi team.

## Using internal resources: some golden rules

Although the internal resources you need will naturally depend on your decisions about using outside consultants, there are some golden rules which apply to every quality management project, however it is designed and carried out. These are:

- make sure senior management is involved, and stays involved

- appoint a quality management representative

- allow enough time in your estimate of resources

- allow enough resources for training.

### *Make sure senior management are involved*

It is unlikely that your quality management project will have got off the ground at all without senior management support. However, just as it may seem tempting to quality management system project managers to let external consultants write the manual, so it often seems very tempting to senior management to hand over the project to middle management at this stage. The result is a manual which does very little to enhance the business, and which is not regarded as very important because senior management clearly don't want to know much about it.

Of course senior management don't have to actually write the quality management manual themselves: it is quite legitimate to delegate tasks such as collecting work instructions, for example, or compiling job descriptions, or analysing the management processes that already exist.

However none of this will help the organisation much if the information that comes out while the manual is being compiled isn't examined in a strategic way. And senior management are the only people who can do this, who have a complete overview of the organisation and who know all about the systems like sales management, or finance and auditing, or personnel, or health and safety, and so on: how well they work, and how they don't. They are also the only people who have a complete view of where they want to go, what is happening in the market-place, what their customers want, future trends, and so on. So they are the only people who can make sure that the quality management manual is taking the organisation where it needs to go, and not down some bureaucratic blind alley.

A good example of this point is purchasing (see section 4.6.2 of ISO9001). In most organisations the purchasing function has to tighten its procedures to conform to the standard. Subcontractors have to be monitored and assessed, so that there are no weak links in the supply chain which jeopardise the quality of the final product.

But the new system has to be made to work strategically. In fact the standard gives room for interpretation just so that this can happen, so that the organisation can decide what it needs from its relationships with its subcontractors and define its controls accordingly.

This doesn't always happen. In one case involving a major utility, a good supplier of many years' standing was left off the approved supplier list because of a technicality (the criteria for the approved suppliers list included achieving a particular financial ratio to indicate viability). The purchasing manager concerned was not aware of this situation for some time, because the decision had been made at a clerical level. The person concerned had done the job and followed procedures. When the situation came to light, the procedures had to be changed so that suppliers could not be left off the list without the purchasing manager being involved to exercise discretion. The ratio which had caused all the trouble in the first place was also dropped.

So, without management oversight to make sure the organisation's aims will be fulfilled and not thwarted by the procedures, things like this will happen and give quality management the reputation it already has in some quarters for counter-productive bureaucracy.

Make sure that senior management set the policy, and that they monitor the progress of the quality management manual as it is drafted. If you feel that you don't have the right level of involvement, think about how you could set about getting it, perhaps using external consultants as a catalyst.

### Appoint a quality management representative

It is a mandatory requirement of the standard to appoint a quality management representative. You must make sure that there is someone in your organisation who knows all about the quality management manual when the input from the quality management consultants is phased out. This may well be the quality management system project manager, or someone who has been given a particular responsibility for the quality management manual. The need for such a role will be more or less obvious depending on how you have managed the project. If you have used external consultants extensively, for example, there is a very real danger that you do not have anyone internal who has an overview of the manual. And the assessors are not going to like that. Quite rightly, they feel it is important to have someone on site who understands what decisions were made, why and how, and who can take on the role of change controller in the years following the quality management manual's introduction.

Quality management representatives can come from a variety of backgrounds, but the qualities they need to have are:

- an understanding of the organisation

- an overview of the quality management system

- good personal skills, such as tact, diplomacy, tenacity, commonsense, creativity.

This person will 'own' the manual and care about what happens to it.

# Choosing a quality management representative

You can be quite creative about where you look for your quality management representative. Consider:

### The trainee

A trainee, perhaps a recent graduate, can make a very useful contribution by taking responsibility for the quality manual. The role provides the trainee with real exposure across the organisation, and a challenging responsibility which will test the newcomer's ability to deliver results.

### Early retirers

The tendency in recent years to slim down the layers of management in organisations and to cut head office staff has made some very experienced and capable individuals redundant in their early fifties. What better role for a senior executive than to take over the quality management representative role?

### A part-time quality management representative

Where a full-time job is not economically feasible, but where there is a real job to be done, you may consider employing a part-time quality management representative. This way of using staff is increasingly popular in, for example, the oil industry, where high-calibre staff are used on a contract basis. One or two days a week may be enough. It is easy to control such an appointment, since the results are very tangible: either you've got a manual, or you haven't.

### Allow enough time

When you are calculating the resources you will need, you must include time for every individual and department that will be involved, in addition to the time that people with particular quality management system responsibilities are going to need. Most of this time will be taken up in departmental meetings and individual interviews, and it will come to quite a large total.

How you find the time depends on the size and nature of your organisation. But don't just shrug your shoulders and hope. If you don't deal with the issue in some way, you will inevitably cause resentment and inefficiency, as you will be asking people to make bricks without straw.

As the training motto says:

> If you can't afford the cost of training, can you afford the cost of ignorance?

For some creative ideas for finding time, look at page 145, 'choosing a quality management representative'.

Other ideas might be:

- using existing training allocations

- employing temporary staff to free up permanent staff

- offering overtime payments

- combining with other management of change projects, such as computerisation, or changing the organisational structure

- cutting management layers

- upgrading management skills

- using a management student in their holiday period.

### Allocate enough resources to training

Training departments in every organisation will tell you that training is never properly planned or resourced. It is true that change management programmes of any kind can absorb an awful lot of training before everyone is confident about the change.

So don't underestimate the amount of training you will need. A typical quality management system training programme would cover topics such as:

- background to quality

- quality management systems

- the quality management manual
- the registration process
- background to audit
- audit checklists
- the audit programme and procedures
- audit technique
- audit reports.

There are a number of sources of training. Traditionally quality management training has come from the consultants who are helping you to implement your quality management system. This has the advantage of tailoring training very precisely to your needs.

There are also short courses on various aspects of quality management. The Institute of Quality Assurance is probably one of the best-known training providers who run short courses on quality management techniques.

Finally, you will start to find national quality management courses and qualifications becoming available, as the demand for quality management training increases. Examples are the BTEC qualifications, the Quality Assurance Certificate, and the Total Quality Management Diploma. This may be an appropriate route for the key quality management role or roles in your organisation.

As the demand for training becomes more widespread, there will undoubtedly be more developments in the training which is available.


## Planning your resources

Now you need to work out a plan for your resources to get the right balance between external consultants and internal resources.

You can put together an overview of the resources you will need by devising a planning checklist which lists the activities which need to happen and who is going to carry them out.

The planning chart we suggest in Figure 36 also has a middle section which asks whether you have the skills and the time to carry out the activities, effectively showing the reasons behind your choice. Using the middle columns gives three options:

- *yes* in both columns: the activity is carried out internally
- *no* in both columns: the activity is carried out by external consultants

*Project management*

- one of each of the responses *yes* or *no* in each column: the activity needs a high level of involvement from both sides.

This chart is also a useful way of presenting your decisions if you have to argue for resources, as it shows the thinking behind your decisions in a detailed way.

This chart also forms the basis for your relationship with your chosen quality management consultants, as it lets them see exactly what you expect them to do. It should enable you to use the resources that are available to you wisely and well.

Figure 36 is an example of a resources planning chart used in a large computer software company. You will need to decide on the precise activities and the level of detail of planning you will need for yourself.

Internal resources

| Activity | Skills | Time | Who does it | How much |
|---|---|---|---|---|
| 1 Initial audit | No | Yes | Consultants | 3 days |
| 2 Agree project objectives | Yes | Yes | Board of directors | 2 days |
| 3 Set scope of registration | No | Yes | Consultants | 0.5 days |
| 4 Prepare draft policy manual | No | Yes | Consultants | 2 days |
| 5 Identify procedures | No | No | Consultants | 2 days |
| 6 Write procedures | Yes | Yes | Department heads | 20 days |
| 7 Awareness training | No | Yes | Consultants | 4 days |
| 8 Desktop check | No | Yes | Consultants | 2 days |
| 9 Identifying Level 3 docs | Yes | Yes | Operations manager | 5 days |
| 10 Launch QMS | Yes | Yes | Senior management | 4 days |
| 11 Audit training | No | No | Consultants | 2 days |
| 12 Auditing | Yes | Yes | Internal auditors | 20 days |
| 13 Assessment application | No | Yes | Consultants | 0.5 days |
| 14 Desktop audit | No | Yes | Assessment body | 1 day |
| 15 Assessment | No | Yes | Assessment body | 3 days |
| 16 Corrections | Yes | Yes | Quality representative | 2 days |

**Figure 36** *Resources planning chart*

# Choosing a quality management consultant

When you have decided what the role of external consultants is to be, you are ready to choose your consultant. Since your relationship with your consultant will be very important and may well determine the success of the project as a whole, choose carefully.

A typical choice will be between:

- a sole practitioner, who has implemented one or two systems

- a large management consultancy, which provides quality as part of its range of services

- a specialist quality management consultancy.

You should look carefully at the experience of the consultancy you are considering. Experience of your industry sector is always useful, because the consultants will be familiar with and sympathetic to the peculiarities of your business and may have useful contacts. On the other hand, some variety of experience is useful too and may lead to a more creative approach.

Ask for references and success rates, and make sure you find out exactly who will be working on your project. It's no good being impressed by the principals of a consultancy, only to find that the particular person assigned to your case does not impress you, or your boss, or the shop floor.

Other points to check are:

- how many days will be spent working on your site

- how much interaction with the consultants you will have at each stage of their work, so that you can retain project control

- what the deliverables will be

- whether the consultants are registered to the quality management standard themselves

- what training they can offer

- what support they can offer after registration to ISO9000.

Finally, check on their manner of working. You should be very wary of any proposal which smacks of a stock solution – the quality technicians who will hand down a solution from on high. Your consultants must know how to work with you, rather than dictating to you.

◆ The Managing Agent for the DTI Quality Initiative is:
Pera International Technology Centre Melton Mowbray Leicestershire LE13 OLX
Tel 0664 501501
Fax 0664 501261

Currently a good source of advice is the Managing Agent for the DTI Quality Initiative. Whether or not you are eligible for a grant, they are usually happy to provide you with the names of two or three consultants with the relevant experience and who have, over a period of years, been vetted for the quality of their work.

## Case Study (i)

### Smith Fraser Ltd – Keeping it Simple

Smith Fraser Ltd is a small company employing 10 staff with a turnover of less than £2 million per annum. Under the direction of its owner-manager, Peter Philips, it sells stationery and computer consumables by catalogue. In June 1991, six months before the catalogue was due for its yearly reprint, Peter Philips decided to go for ISO9000 registration.

Peter Philips decided to use a quality management consultancy since with so few staff Smith Fraser didn't have the resources to carry out the necessary work itself. His brief to the consultants was a standard one in most respects. Philips wanted the consultants to carry out an initial audit, design a quality management system, and implement it. The only unusual part of the brief was the timescale – six months from project start to registration. Philips wanted certification by the catalogue's reprint deadline, so that he could use the registered firm symbol in it.

Although in theory it was possible to work to this deadline, the consultants were realistic, since experience had taught them that in any given company things were seldom as simple as they seemed. The system might not be customer-focused, for example, or the computer system might have to be extended to provide proper controls, or the staff might turn out to be rather less co-operative than the project's sponsor.

However, Peter Philips promised his full support and was so insistent about achieving the six-months goal that the consultants agreed to put together a plan to achieve it, spelling out clearly the level of co-operation they would have to have from Smith Fraser.

The resulting project was a model of speed and efficiency. Because Peter Philips had been pursuing an aggressive Customer First policy for many years, the management systems in place at Smith Fraser were already finely tuned to customers' needs. Some further fine-tuning was inevitable, but really the systems in place needed very little alteration to meet the requirements of the quality management standard. And because Philips ran his company professionally, his staff quickly adapted to any changes in the systems and procedures and were able to build up the record of three months' compliance with the quality management manual that they needed for registration.

The project started on 21 June 1991. System design occurred in June and July, with implementation as an ongoing activity. Bedding in the system took place in August and September, followed by three months during which the company could demonstrate the necessary period of compliance. Registration was achieved almost exactly six months later, on 15 December. Although the catalogue reprint was already under way by this time, there was still just time to place the registered firm symbol on the cover and on the interior title pages. Peter Philips had achieved his goal.

The costs for this project were surprisingly low. Smith Fraser applied for and received a DTI initiative support grant, and because so little had to be changed, the total costs to the company for the consultancy were only £3,200.

Smith Fraser was able to achieve registration so painlessly because it was so well prepared. The company had clear business objectives, clear policies and sound management. All that ISO9000 did was to pull the threads together and provide a blueprint for the continued success of the company. In the present climate of business failures, such companies make a refreshing change.

## Case Study (ii)

### Autocomponents UK Ltd – Building on the Culture

Autocomponents UK is the UK branch of a US parent company, the Autocomponents Corporation, which manufactures automotive components and which is famous as an example of one of the US's excellent companies with an outstanding commitment to quality and customer service. Autocomponents UK, with a staff of 200 and a multi-million pound turnover, shares the strongly quality-oriented culture of its US parent. This culture is made explicit in a list of 40 guiding principles and has helped the company to survive challenges and threats from changing market conditions.

In December 1990, Autocomponents UK decided to go for ISO9000 registration to add yet another strand to its quality programme. Autocomponents brought in a team of quality management consultants to lead this work, but also allocated substantial internal resources to the project, for liaising with the consultants, for training and for auditing the implementation.

Autocomponents had good quality attitudes deep in its culture, but these had not always been made explicit as formal procedures. There was a lot of work to be done in formally defining processes and in persuading first line managers in particular to buy in. Where necessary working practices were changed to achieve consistency as well as effectiveness. The key to success lay in translating the requirements of the ISO9000 standard into Autocomponents' own language, so that the strong culture that already existed worked for quality management and not in opposition to it.

Autocomponents UK was successful in gaining registration, although the process of merging the quality management standard with the existing culture did take some time to achieve. Consultancy costs were just under £20,000. Autocomponents used external consultancy time efficiently by setting up a strong internal project management system and by having a receptive culture which made the most of the management consultants' advice.

# Case Study (iii)
## Franklin West Ltd – Making it Complicated

Franklin West Ltd is a small contracting business with 14 employees. In November 1990 the owner of the company decided to take the time to go to a quality management presentation being given jointly by the DTI and a quality management consultancy. Throughout the presentation this man sat quietly taking notes and nodding knowledgeably from time to time when particular points arose.

At the end of the presentation, participants were asked for their questions and reactions. These were mostly very positive. But suddenly, the owner of Franklin West spoke up.

'I've only one thing to say to you lot here today,' he said. 'You'd better be bloody careful about who you get and what you tell them to do. There are only 14 of us in our company, but now we've got a manual that must be over 100 pages long and a bill for £80,000. And we're no nearer registration than we were a year ago. I tell you, it's like writing a blank cheque, getting in consultants. I can't see any end to it at all. We can't back out now, or we'd lose what we've put in. But who's to say how long it's going to take?'

There was a shocked silence in the room as the participants silently considered the consequences to their own businesses of a bill for £80,000. And everyone was reaching the same conclusion: they simply couldn't afford the risk.

The quality management consultant leading the presentation could see that all the good work of the morning had been undone at a stroke. Taking his courage in both hands, he said:

> 'Well, if that's the case you've been taken for a ride. Let's see. As a guide, we'd say that for a company of about 15 people, the quality policy manual is going to be about 10 to 20 pages long, the quality procedures manual is going to be about 30 to 40 pages long, and the workplace references usually exist anyway. With a DTI grant, that should cost you up to £5000. We'd suggest about 15 days for the initial audit, planning the project, deciding on the system model and the registration body, and designing and writing down the complete system. Then you'd need 5 days' training and implementation support. You shouldn't need more.
> Why don't you tell us all exactly what happened to you?'

Franklin West's story was simple. The company's owner had decided to go for ISO9000 registration. He had asked his secretary to look up some names of quality management consultancies for him and she had come up with a name. He didn't know how she had found it. 'Probably from the Yellow Pages,' he reflected.

The management consultants had been told to write a quality management manual. The owner of Franklin West admitted that the consultants had been doing that: there was a draft manual inches thick sitting on everyone's desk. He had not much idea where the procedures in the manual had come from. He was sure they were very good, but he was also sure that he didn't understand them, and that no one else in the organisation did either. The consultants were going to have to spend weeks explaining them to everybody, and then re-writing them, and so it would go on.

At this point the adviser from the DTI stepped in. His advice was short and to the point. Franklin West should stop what it was doing and start again. This time, before spending their money, they should define what they really wanted from an outside consultancy. Bringing in outsiders with such an open-ended brief was a certain recipe for disaster. The quality management consultants, lacking any other direction, had set about creating the kind of bureaucratic system they were familiar with from their work with some of the larger contractors. But as Franklin West's owner was beginning to realise, this was not the kind of system that he needed.

Franklin West's owner had learned a lot the hard way about how not to use outside consultants. He was able to rescue some of the work from the initial investment, in the form of detailed work instructions which had been documented very thoroughly. However, all of the quality policy manual and the quality procedures manual had to be started again before Franklin West had the kind of quality management system it understood and could operate effectively.

# Preparing the Quality Management Manual 10

In this chapter we look in some detail at the activities which relate directly to preparing the quality management manual. Remember, there are no definitively right or wrong ways of doing things, as long as you end up with the result you want. If you have a very clear plan you are quite likely to succeed even if it doesn't altogether follow conventional wisdom, as happened with Smith Fraser, the company in the first case study at the end of Chapter 9.

## Key stages in the project

Key stages in producing the manual are:

- collecting information
- drafting the quality management manual
- completing an internal desktop check or audit
- setting up long-term control procedures
- issuing the quality management manual.

These stages form the set-up phase of the project. There are in addition longer-term activities which are described in Chapter 11, *Assessment and After*.

## Collecting information

A significant part of the quality manual project consists of collecting information: either information which already exists in some form around the organisation, or which needs to be provided specially for the manual. There are a number of techniques which can be used to gather this information. The main ones are:

- individual interviews

- group discussions

- questionnaires

- observation.

### Individual interviews

◆ Key points to cover might be:
– the tasks the person does
– the paperwork they have to fill in
– how these tasks are placed in the time-line
– any duplication
– the place of computers
– any problems or suggestions.

Since the purpose of the manual is to write down and formalise what people do, it makes a lot of sense to start by asking people individually what that is. You should not be too prescriptive in these interviews, at least not initially. On the other hand, you should interview consistently. Make a checklist of the key things you have to cover, structuring the interview around the way in which the paperwork is processed. This will give you a point of reference to return to when one topic is exhausted.

Interviews are very economical in time for the interviewee and are generally regarded much more favourably than, for example, requests for a written response. Also people find it interesting to talk about what they do and will probably be very informative. One word of warning though: be aware that you do need to keep the interview on track; don't let the discussion wander too far from the point.

You might consider taping your interviews. Taking notes can slow you down and cause you to miss important parts of what's being said. People tend to think they will find the idea of being taped inhibiting, but in practice they soon forget all about the microphone and talk quite normally. If you have enough secretarial support, you can have transcripts typed up from the tapes, but if you haven't, it's perfectly possible just to take notes from the tape.

### Group discussions

Of course individual interviews, while they are economical in time for the interviewee, are very extravagant in time for the interviewer. You end up telling everyone individually about what you're doing. In an organisation of any size, it isn't feasible to carry out one-to-one interviews with everyone, within acceptable time and resource limits.

Another problem with individual interviews is that you will find that different people have different perceptions of their organisation. These differences may reflect major differences in policy, as in the case study at the end of Chapter 4, which will become obvious to the interviewer. These differences will have to be resolved jointly.

This doesn't mean that you should ignore the experience and ideas of individuals, however. It really can't be emphasised enough how important it is to make sure not only that everyone in the organisation knows about quality management developments, but that the quality manual project team knows what's going on in the business.

The way round this problem is to reserve one-to-one interviewing for people in key roles, and to talk to all the employees who share roles or functions in groups. However, be warned: group discussions can be quite lively, and they can also be off the point. The chairperson will need to keep a firm grip on proceedings to focus the meetings and to sidetrack ruthlessly all those interesting but irrelevant discussions about the politics of the workplace.

If you have either experienced problems like this or feel that you might be heading that way, the chairperson role could be one for an outside consultant. The quality management consultant will, from experience, have a clear idea of how the meetings should go and also, if you have chosen well, have plenty of responses to difficult questions up his or her sleeve, based on experience and good case studies.

## Questionnaires

Questionnaires are useful for collecting factual responses, which can then be analysed statistically. Be aware, however, that supposedly factual responses can be subjective. People may think they know something and record it as a fact, and yet be wrong. A good way to deal with this in the design of your questionnaire is to follow each question with a certainty question (see example): this will give you a good indication of the information that needs checking.

Even if your questionnaire is strictly factual, you should still put in one or two open-ended questions. For example, if you are asking people about what manuals they use, you could end the questionnaire by asking:

*What is the best thing about the manuals?*
*What is the worst thing about the manuals?*

This gives people the opportunity to tell you all the things you hadn't thought of asking, and at the same time prevents comments degenerating into a general moan by insisting on positive comments as well as negative ones. Open-ended questions can't be processed statistically, but, like the certainty count,

◆ **Certainty**
How certain are you that your answer is right?
[   ] Very certain
[   ] Quite certain
[   ] Not sure

◆ **Multiple question**
Do you need to see New Scientist and/or any other periodical when it comes out, and do you know where to find it/them?
**Single questions**
Do you need to see New Scientist?
[ ] No [ ] Yes
Do you need to see any other periodicals?
*If you do, list them here.*
[ ] No [ ] Yes
.............................
Do you know where to find magazines you want?
[ ] No [ ] Yes
[ ] Sometimes

they will give you a good indication of which issues need to be followed up.

Finally, make sure that your questions are easy to understand. Don't use multiple questions, which ask more than one question at a time. Just have one point per question. Also, avoid questions which are rather long because you are explaining the question at the same time as you are asking it. Explanations are really notes which can be separated out from the main question. And make sure you always leave enough space for the answer.

## Observation

Observation is a technique which is used extensively in auditing quality management systems. It is really auditing, or in this case information gathering, by walking about. Keep an eye open for:

- *anything pinned to a notice board.* Quality management is not management by notice boards: if information is held there because it is important and needs to be accessible, there should be a proper place for it in the quality management system.

- *sticky notes and old envelopes.* The same argument as for notice-boards applies to yellow stickies and old envelopes. There has to be a system for recording important messages and phone numbers, which makes sure they don't get thrown in the bin. Sticky notes are a great idea for reminders, or for putting down temporary information, but they absolutely shouldn't be used for anything important or long term. Hands up everyone who has ended up at the end of the day searching through their waste paper bin in a state of mounting panic, muttering 'I know I wrote it down somewhere...'.

- *filled-in forms.* You will quickly see what parts people leave out or perhaps what information gets added in. People get used to forms and can carry on for years quite happily making the best of redundant questions and obscure layouts. They may not really have noticed the problems, in which case it is up to the observer to see how things could be improved.

- *manuals and reference books at people's work stations.* These are the documents which make up the workplace references. Make a note of what you find, and compare it with the lists you will collect about what people think they need.

- *manuals and reference books* not *at people's work stations*. You are quite likely to come across reference materials which everyone needs but which have somehow never been properly provided. Clues to these are probably verbal, as in 'Does anyone have a copy of...?'.

# Drafting the quality manual

In Chapters 7 and 8 we looked at how to apply writing and design skills to the information in the quality manual, to transform it into a usable document. Here we look at how to decide who should do this work. This decision will, of course, have to fit in with your overall resourcing policy, as described in Chapter 9, *Planning and Resourcing the Project*.

The choice is emphatically not a simple matter of whether you have anyone with the time to do the drafting or not. Rather the issues you should consider are:

- the degree of customisation of the ISO9000 standard that you will need

- the level of writing and design skills that you have.

### *The degree of customisation of the ISO9000 standard that you will need*

This will be determined by the nature of your industry and by the kind of organisation you are. All manuals are necessarily unique. Nevertheless some industry sectors clearly relate to the standard more straightforwardly than others, and within industries some organisational structures will be easier to define than others.

You may think that the more customisation that is needed, the more difficult the project will be and the more outside help you will need. This is true, but in fact it is also true that a non-standard manual means that you and your organisation will need to be closely involved with developing a suitable quality management model, as outsiders won't really be able to adapt one effectively. So if it's going to be difficult, you'll have to spend time on it.

On the other hand, a more standard manual is much easier for outside experts to develop for you, because the experts have done it many times before and will be quick and efficient. So if it's going to be relatively straightforward, someone else can do more of it.

▲ Traditionally large manufacturing industries related very closely to the published standard. Service businesses were the ones which had to look at the principles underlying the standard, and adapt those principles to their systems. However with the decline in the manufacturing sector, more and more companies are turning to newer and more flexible structures to stay alive. This means adapting the standard even for manufacturing industries.

### *The level of writing and design skills you have*

The problem with writing is that it is a skill which we all use, so it is tempting to think that finding someone to write the standards is going to be quite easy. But there are actually surprisingly few people who can write clearly and effectively, especially where complex instructional material is involved. This is as true, incidentally, of management consultants as it is of the people in your organisation.

If you decide you want help with writing, some companies offer a service in procedures writing and structural editing. They can either revise what you have written, or draft out the manual from any notes and instructions you have put together.

## The desktop check or audit

After the manual has been drafted, there will be loose ends to tie together, such as:

- gaps in references
- duplicated procedures
- contradictory procedures
- gaps in conformance with the standard.

These loose ends need to be sorted out before the completed first draft can be issued to staff, and certainly before the manual can be submitted for assessment.

The process of checking that the quality manual (and by logical extension, the quality system itself) conforms with the ISO9000 standard is known as the *desktop check* or *audit*. This process involves reading each requirement of the standard line by line, understanding its logical meaning and possible interpretations of it, and checking that it is covered and explicitly referenced by the quality manual. It is a sensible idea to do the desktop check at the same time as filling in the conformance table at the end of the quality policy manual.

The desktop check need not take a very long time, but it is essential that it is thorough – very thorough – as the verdict of the ISO9000 assessor on whether or not your system meets the standard will depend on how well you do it. Because of the expertise required, this exercise suggests itself as one where the experts will play a strong supporting role. You can and should have your own copy of the ISO9000 standard to work from, but the consultant's eye will be much more perceptive that your own in picking up any gaps and discords between your manual and the quality standard.

The desktop check is a good point to take stock of the project as a whole, to take an overview of the draft quality management manual and to be satisfied that you have identified all the procedures that you want to establish as the cornerstone of your quality management system, and have not included anything that you would rather not formalise.

---

## Desktop check report

*This is an extract from an actual desktop audit carried out for the client by a quality management consultancy. The comments refer to procedures which the consultant is not entirely happy about.*

**Sales procedure**

Where is the quotation procedure? Contract review has two elements:

1. Quotation
2. Order processing

The Sales Procedure states: 'So details of the review will be dependent on the value or complexity of the order.'

This is too vague and leaves the interpretation up to the individual. The system should provide the parameters, otherwise the ISO9000 assessor will suspect there is no system and go into some detail to check. Maybe it would be better not to raise this?

Similar the Sales Procedure states: 'Records must be made and retained for all Contract Reviews'.

What records?
Retained where?
Who makes them?

Again, this is not clear and opens up a range of questions.

Finally the Sales Procedure states: 'A meeting is held daily between the production manager and the sales supervision to discuss…'.

If this is stated in the procedure, it will be subject to audit. Is this desirable? Is it a prime control mechanism? Is it for information only?

**Calibration**

Why is equipment not included in the calibration system? This needs to be explained to the assessors. As a general principle, the procedure should answer the question before it is asked. This is a good example. It is certain that the ISO9000 assessors will spend some time at a detailed level on this procedure. The statement that some things are not in the system begs the question why? On whose authority is it in or out?

# Controlling the quality manual

All parts of the quality manual have to be under what the standard refers to as document control: it's one of the disciplines of quality management which will automatically apply to the quality manual itself. Think how embarrassing it's going to be, if you don't practise the document control procedures you preach in the manual...

■ See section 4.5 of ISO9000 (1987).

You will need to have your document control system in place as soon as you have completed the desktop audit, and before you issue the first draft to staff for training and implementation. The elements of a document control system are:

- issue number

- copy number

- date

- page numbers

- authorisation

- management standard reference base

- circulation list

- issue status and review log.

The first five items should appear on every page of the manual.

Remember that document control details apply to each part of the quality management manual and the workplace references, if the manual is issued in separate parts. There are many ways of achieving document control. Figure 37 shows how you might approach the document control for the first two parts of the quality management manual.

# Issuing the quality manual

When you are satisfied that the draft quality manual is complete and conforms to the ISO9000 standard, it is time to issue the manual and start to train your employees.

You will now have to decide who should have a copy of the manual. Opinions differ about this. Some companies like to give everyone a copy, works cat included. For example, one large multinational has the quality manual produced as an insert to a time management diary system, with every employee having their own personal copy. This is very expensive, of course, and you will have great difficulty in controlling all the copies,

---

## Company PQR Ltd

Quality Manual BS 5750: Part 2: 1987/ISO 9002

Draft 1

Copy number 4

Date  1.8.91

Page 1 of 1

Authorised by...........................................

---

**Circulation list**

| Copy number | Issued to | Position/department |
|---|---|---|
| 1 | John Brown | MD |
| 2 | Susan Brown | Financial controller |
| 3 | Terry Green | Retail manager |
| 4 | Michelle Blue | Buyer |
| | | |

---

**Issue status and review log**

| Section | Sub-Section | Page | Issue | Amendment | Date | Signed |
|---|---|---|---|---|---|---|
| | | | | | | |
| | | | | | | |
| | | | | | | |
| | | | | | | |

**Figure 37** *Document control information*

particularly when changes start to come in. But for this particular company this policy works well.

At the other extreme other companies don't issue enough copies so that the quality management system remains a well-kept secret.

A sensible, middle-ground option is to provide each key function with a copy. That way, distribution will be limited, but everyone will know where to find a copy of the manual.

## Training your users

You will probably have had in place an ongoing training and awareness programme as part of the implementation of your quality management system (see Chapter 9, *Planning and Resourcing the Project*). As part of this programme you need to arrange company-wide sessions to introduce and explain the manual to everyone in the organisation. How you do this depends on the size of your company, of course. Unless you are small enough to fit everyone in one room, the most obvious way to organise training is by function.

Training which is specifically about using the quality manual is necessary to make sure that everyone has the chance to take time out to become familiar with the procedures and to think through what this will mean for them as individuals. Ideally everyone will be able to internalise the new ways of doing things before the starting date for the new procedures. In practice this is unlikely, and you should plan to provide support materials for some time after the manual comes into use.

## Using training aids

As a follow-up to the training sessions you have held to familiarise staff with the quality manual, you may want to use training aids for people to use at their work stations to remind them of the new procedures and help them learn the procedures more quickly – something to look at when a telephone call is being put through, for example. These can be very effective and significantly reduce the amount of time people need to get familiar with the manual.

However, you can only do this for a limited period of time – at most, until formal assessment day. There is a good reason for this, of course: these training aids are not controlled and will not be automatically updated when there are changes to the manual. So make sure they are all removed as soon as people have had a chance to learn the system. If you don't, dusty and ear-marked

◆ Training aids could be:
– flow-charts
– reminder notices, for example on the order book (have you filled in the pink form?)
– procedure summaries in large letters
– posters and charts.

copies will return to haunt you years later, as somebody discovers and adopts an alternative version of a procedure which you thought you had finished with a long time ago.

### Establishing the authority of the quality manual

Once the first issue of the manual is in circulation, it becomes the only authority that people should use. This point will have been made in the training sessions you held to introduce the quality manual. In practice, insisting on the sole authority of the quality manual can be quite difficult.

When you were collecting information for the manual, you looked at the informal systems people used to help them with their jobs and at the workplace instructions that had to be in place. Now, you are telling people to stop using the very systems they evolved to help them with their jobs in the first place. Often this can seem like a personal intrusion, as well as an erosion of the all-important entrepreneurial spirit of the business. People won't always recognise that it is anybody's business but their own if they like to write messages on yellow stickies and put them on other people's computers, or if they like to have particular points of information close to hand stuck up on the notice-board or taped to the work-bench.

However, the survival of these apparently harmless little habits could quite easily jeopardise your chances of registration. An individual using a system that is not documented or a system that should have been phased out is regarded as a major example of non-compliance by the assessors. It is evidence that your formal system doesn't cover or control all your critical activities, and that you have not managed to change the culture of the organisation from informal to formal.

Once again the accounts department is a good example of this point. When a business starts up you will put in financial systems which are audited every year to make sure you are using them properly. Once you have established your accounts system you can change it, but only if everyone in the business agrees and if the changes are within accounting conventions. You can't just make changes as you feel like it, or take short-cuts because you are short of time.

So be ruthless in establishing the sole authority of the quality manual. Mobilise a group of document police to seek out and destroy all the things that shouldn't be there – the envelopes with important addresses jotted down on them, old conversion tables, the drawings stuck on the work-bench. One particularly common area of non-compliance is in the purchasing department, where

◆ One major multi-national has as its slogan:
*Work to the system or work to have the system changed.*

the buyer may not be using the approved supplier list, but using instead old business cards, a local directory of suppliers, the Yellow Pages, a calendar, and so on.

Once you have removed all the old paperwork, forms, drawings and previous procedures, people will then have no alternative but to learn how to use the formal system instead of their private one. Who knows, they may even find it an improvement.

Establishing the authority of the quality manual can actually be quite awkward if the challenger is one of the senior managers. This is another reason why quality management systems which don't have top management support are doomed to failure. The most common scenario is where senior management make a decision which necessitates a change in procedures – let's say the company decides to put signing authorities on its purchasing procedure. The managing director will immediately do what has always been done in these circumstances: issue a memo to all departments. When this happens, you will have to remind the MD that changes in procedures have to be incorporated in the quality management manual, and follow whatever change system you have set up. Hopefully you will meet with a positive response...

## Preparing for assessment

When you are confident that the quality manual has taken hold, and that its procedures have been followed for three months, the set-up phase of the quality manual project is over. You are well on the way to the big test: external assessment. After all the planning, hard work and expense, the end is in sight. You are about to become (hopefully) a registered organisation.

## Case Study

### *Jordans Ltd – Managing a Successful Project*

Jordans Ltd employs 800 staff and has a turnover of around £70 million. It designs and manufactures industrial and commercial racking and shelving systems.

Towards the end of the 1980s the management decided to respond to the increasing interest in ISO9000 and implement a quality management system. Jordans decided not to use consultants, using instead their structural engineering department. After all, these were the people who were most concerned with product quality. They had attended meetings about the standard, organised through their Chamber of Commerce, and seemed to be the ideal choice for running the project. Work proceeded at a steady pace and in October 1987 Jordans applied for assessment, and failed.

In January 1988 Harry Smith had just arrived at work when the phone rang. It was his old friend David James. A number of years ago, Harry and David had worked together in production for a large multinational chemical company. Both men had since moved on: Harry was now a quality management consultant, while David had stayed in production. However, they still kept in touch, meeting up about twice a year to keep up to date and to swap stories about their jobs.

It was unusual for David to ring Harry during working hours. He explained:

> I've just got this new job Harry. It's with Jordans – I'm their new production manager. I'm really excited about it, but I'm just beginning to realise that it's a bit of a hot spot. The previous chap resigned in a hurry last October when Jordans didn't make it through ISO9000 registration, after two years on the project.
> Now everyone's looking at me to see if I can do it. Can you help?

Harry and David were not just friends because of social reasons. They shared the same attitudes towards their work, particularly the same concern for quality. So Harry knew that David would not just be concerned about getting ISO9000 registration to save face, but also because he understood the benefits of operating a successful quality management system. Harry immediately agreed to help his friend. He knew the assignment was something of a risk, because everyone would be watching the new team with scepticism, and there would be no room for error. However, Harry trusted David and his own abilities enough to decide to accept the challenge.

Harry's first job when he arrived at Jordans later that week was to look over the assessor's report. This stated that the quality system, as expressed in the quality manual, was:

- too complex
- not in line with the requirements of the standard
- not understood and implemented across the company
- not properly controlled.

Harry's heart sank as he read the report. It was pretty damaging. It meant he would have to start all over again to produce a quality manual which actually represented what people did, and which conformed to the standard.

Then David dropped another bombshell. The board of directors were severely embarrassed by Jordans' failure to register in the previous year. They wanted speedy results now, so that the company could recover from the blow to its morale and reputation as quickly as possible. Their deadline was July 1988, just six months away.

Harry put his anxieties behind him and worked out a plan of attack. There wasn't time to start all over again, and anyway most of the groundwork had been done – indeed overdone in some cases. What he needed to do now was to find a way of getting the manual into line with the requirements of the ISO9000 standard on the one hand, and with what people were actually doing on the other. It would then be down to an intensive period of training to ensure compliance in time for the formal assessment.

Harry decided the most efficient way forward would be to hold an intensive series of meetings. Each meeting would deal with one of the requirements of the standard and would be attended by everyone involved in the relevant part of the business. Harry chaired each of these meetings himself, so that time wasn't lost going over old ground and the problems of the past. It was important for morale, as well as for his timescale, not to dwell on the mistakes of the past, but to look forward positively to the future. Harry made sure that the meetings kept to the point and that the requirements of the standard were properly understood.

At the end of each meeting, Harry gave one or two people the task of drafting procedures to reflect what had been discussed in the meeting. Harry then collected all these procedures together and redrafted the manual. He could now be sure that the manual conformed to the ISO9000 standard and that all the procedures in it had been discussed, agreed and understood by the people concerned.

Now Harry had to think of the quickest and most effective way of implementing the quality manual. He decided that the best way would be to get as many people as he could involved in auditing their own processes and procedures: each group of workers could take responsibility themselves for seeing that the procedures were being carried out. Harry arranged for over 200 staff, about 25 per cent of the workforce, to undergo basic audit training.

The day for changing over to the new procedures arrived. Harry had been worried that there would be a gloomy atmosphere, with the memory of the previous failure still fresh in people's minds. But now there was a feeling of confidence. Everyone knew what they had to do, and the newly trained auditors were poised throughout the company to observe and report on how the implementation was going. Within three weeks Harry had his first complete set of audit reports. He then discussed all instances of non-conformance with his auditors and agreed what corrective action should be take. It was then up to the auditors to make sure the corrective action went through.

By July, Harry was exhausted but quietly confident. David had kept him aware of the feedback from both the shop floor and from senior management throughout the period. Some people thought he was going too far too fast, but most were very impressed by the energetic and focused way he had driven the project through.

Jordans did achieve accreditation to ISO9000, and on time. The workforce was very proud of its achievement and senior management were delighted with their new production manager. As for Harry, he collected his fee and took a holiday. It was one time in his life when he could honestly say he deserved it.

# Assessment and After: Maintaining and Developing the Quality Management Manual

# 11

## Introduction

In this chapter we look firstly at the process of presenting your quality management manual for formal assessment, and then at the processes of maintaining and developing the manual for as long as the company exists or maintains its commitment to quality management.

It is important to emphasise that the development of the quality management manual doesn't end with registration for ISO9000, but simply moves into a different phase. Too many organisations stop thinking about the content of the manual once it is formally passed by the ISO9000 assessors, forgetting that their organisations will continue to change and develop and that therefore the first issue of the quality management manual will sooner or later be out of date. If you try to hold your organisation to a set of standards which don't apply any more, you will quickly find yourself disillusioned with ISO9000, as your quality management manual becomes bureaucratic and deadens rather than contributes to your growth and development. Remember always that your objective is to use the system to add value to your business.

▲ The principle of checking out how things are working and changing them where necessary is known as *continuous improvement.*

## About assessment

The official life of the quality management manual starts with its assessment for the ISO9000 quality management standard. Assessment is the process by which, in order to gain registration to ISO9000, your commitment to quality management is inspected and validated. Assessment isn't just a one-off occasion either: after you have been registered to the standard, you can and will be visited at regular intervals to make sure that you are

▲ Periodic assessments cost about the same as a financial audit. In fact it is interesting to speculate about whether chartered accountants will start to move into this market, as the demand for assessment continues to grow.

still conforming to the quality management standards as defined in your quality management manual. It is perfectly possible to have registration withdrawn, if you are not.

To set the assessment process in motion you need, first of all, to choose a certification body.

## Certification bodies

Certification bodies provide assessors who will carry out an assessment process to test your readiness for registration to the standard.

In the early days of the standard assessors were necessarily recruited from the large manufacturing organisations which had sector schemes, and naturally brought with them expectations of how quality management systems should work based on their experience of these large, bureaucratic environments. This traditional approach still exists in some of the certification bodies today, but be careful: you should only use them if the culture of your organisation is compatible with this approach.

Today there are many more certification bodies for specific industries that you can choose from, so you should be able to find an assessor who will consider sympathetically the way in which you have interpreted ISO9000 to suit the culture and management processes of your organisation.

Remember that the role of the certification body is essentially to check that you are controlling your business in the way that you have decided is best for you — not to impose an alien standard. And remember also: the assessor isn't always right. You know your business best, after all. If you are sure of your ground, stand firm and bring the assessor round to your point of view.

Many organisations approach assessment in total fear of the assessors. But they are not there to fail you. They must be satisfied that you conform to the standard and that you deserve their mark of approval, but they won't deliberately try to catch you out.

## The accreditation of certification bodies

Certification bodies are controlled by a process known as accreditation. This is administered by the NACCB (the National Accreditation Council of Certification Bodies) which is an agency under the Department of Trade and Industry. It uses the 'tick and crown' symbol to indicate its approval (see Figure 38).

**Figure 38** *The NACCB tick and crown symbol*

The accreditation of a certification body is not a blanket approval, but is based on industry sectors. There is a 'chicken and egg' situation, whereby the certification body needs to have registered at least five or six companies before it can become accredited for that industry sector. Once it is accredited, the certification body can award both the ISO9000 registration symbol and the NACCB accreditation symbol.

Clearly in an industry sector which is just beginning to take an interest in ISO9000, none of the certification bodies will be able to gain accreditation straight away. In this situation they can award ISO9000 as an interim measure, with the accreditation symbol to follow once they have established a track record. Ultimately all industry sectors will be covered either by an accredited specialist certification body, or by one of the larger multi-sector bodies with a wide range of accredited sectors.

# Choosing a certification body

◆ Quality management consultants can help you with this: in fact many will keep up-to-date records for their staff anyway, and be able to advise you on who to consider, how long they take, when to register and what they cost.

Finding the right certification body will be important for you, so you should go about it in much the same way as you would to find the right quality management consultant.

You should check first of all to see if there is a certification body for your industry, and use it if there is. You can approach first of all the NACCB, who will tell you which assessors for your industry have been accredited by them. If there aren't any, then you will have to do some homework.

You might try other sources of information such as trade associations or other technical, legal or professional services to which you have access. Also ask around informally to see if there are any widely held views about the certification bodies for your industry.

Another approach is to contact the certification bodies direct to find out who can demonstrate the specific industry expertise you are looking for. You may find a clear market leader, or three or four with some experience in your field.

If you still draw a blank, talk to each of the certification bodies about the kind of quality management system you are developing. Not all will be interested: shortlist the ones who are.

## *Fees*

Each certification body publishes its own fee structure. These don't vary greatly, but there can be quite a difference in daily rates, which will affect on-costs after assessment and registration have been completed.

The total size of the bill will depend very much on the size of your organisation (for obvious reasons, as there will be a lot more work involved for larger organisations). For example, in their 1992 price list one certification body quotes a figure of between £3500 and £4000 for assessing a company of up to 30 employees. This charge rises to £8000 for a company of up to 250 employees.

The initial assessment fee will cover the following stages in the assessment process:

- document review

- the assessment visit

- report and recommendations

- corrective action

- approval and registration to ISO9000.

If you fail either at the document review or at assessment, the relevant part of the process will be repeated. You will have to pay for this, but only for the extra time you take: you don't have to start at the beginning again each time.

After you have made it successfully through initial assessment and registration to the standard, there will be on-costs for:

- surveillance visits (on average two or three times per year)

- whole system review visits (every three years; not offered by all certification bodies)

- revisits (if there are problems).

Looking at costs certainly makes one point very clear: success is going to be a lot cheaper than failure.

# NACCB accredited certification bodies

*Associated Offices Quality
Certification*
Longridge House
Longridge Place
Manchester M60 4DT
Tel: 061 833 2295

*ASTA Certification Services*
Prudential Chambers
23/24 Market Place
Rugby
Warwickshire CV21 3DU
Tel: 0788 578435

*British Standards Institute*
BSI Quality Assurance
PO Box 375
Milton Keynes MK14 6LL
Tel: 0908 220908

*British Approvals Service for
Electric Cables*
Silbury Court
360 Silbury Boulevard
Milton Keynes MK9 2AF
Tel: 0908 691121

*Bureau Veritas Quality
International*
70 Borough High Street
London SE1 1XF
Tel: 071 378 8113

*Central Certification Service Ltd
(CCS)*
Victoria House
Wellingborough
Northants NN8 1LU
Tel: 0933 441796

*Ceramic Industry Certification
Scheme (CICS)*
Queens Road
Penkhull
Stoke on Trent ST4 7LQ
Tel: 0782 411008

*Construction Quality Assurance
(CQA)*
Arcade Chambers
The Arcade
Market Place
Newark
Nottingham NG24 1UD
Tel: 0636 708700

*Det Norske Veritas Quality
Assurance*
Veritas House
112 Station Road
Sidcup
Kent DA15 7BY
Tel: 081 309 7477

*Engineering Inspection
Authorities Board (EIAB)*
1 Birdcage Walk
London SW1H 9JS
Tel: 071 222 7899

*Lloyds Register Quality Assurance
(LRQA)*
Norfolk House
Wellesley Road
Croydon
Surrey CR2 2DT
Tel: 081 688 6882

*National Quality Assurance
(NQA)*
5 Cotswold Business Park
Millfield Lane
Caddington
Luton LU1 4AR
Tel: 0582 841144

*NACOSS*
Queensgate House
14 Cookham Road
Maidenhead
Berkshire SL6 8AJ
Tel: 0628 37572

*SIRA Certification Services*
Saighton Lane
Saighton
Chester CH3 6EG
Tel: 0628 37572

*Loss Prevention Certification
Board*
Melrose Avenue
Borehamwood
Herts WD6 2BJ
Tel: 081 207 2345

*Quality Scheme for Ready Mix
Concrete*
3 High Street
Hampton
Middlesex TW12 2SQ
Tel: 081 941 0273

*TRADA Quality Assurance
Services*
Stocking Lane
Hughenden Valley
High Wycombe
Buckinghamshire HP14 4NR
Tel: 024024 5484

*UK Certification Authority for
Reinforcing Steels*
Oak House
Tubs Hill
Sevenoaks
Kent TN13 1BL
Tel: 0732 450000

*Yarsley Quality Assured Firms*
Trowers Way
Redhill
Surrey RH1 2JN
Tel: 0737 765070

For further details contact:
NACCB
3 Birdcage Walk
London SW1H 9JH
Tel: 071 222 5374

# Working with your assessors

Once you have chosen your certification body, the assessment process can begin. Throughout this process it is important to understand what the assessors are trying to do and how you can help the process along. Think of dealing with the assessors as being like dealing with your tax or VAT inspector. These officials are working to a defined set of rules, but it is often a matter of judgement as to whether or not what you are doing complies with those rules. Compliance sounds like a black-and-white issue, but in reality there is considerable potential for negotiation.

One such example occurred recently when the assessor of a software house thought that company cars should be included under the ISO9000 purchasing policy and procedures. The company in this case argued successfully that company cars had no bearing on the end product of the business, and were therefore not covered by the standard.

And then there was the assessor who picked up a roll of sticky tape and demanded to know what its shelf-life was and whether it was traceable to source....

So don't be surprised, or alarmed or frustrated if you find yourself arguing with your assessor at various points in the assessment process. This is part of a process of understanding and compromise, with each side putting forward their view. Sometimes your view will be accepted, sometimes not.

◆ How to deal with your assessor:
- keep to time
- make sure key staff are available
- KISS: keep it sweet and simple
- keep to the point: don't give your life history
- say if you don't understand the question
- say if you don't know the answer: don't try and bluff
- refer to your manager, if in doubt
- you're the expert — speak with confidence
- argue your corner — politely
- be prepared to accept minor non-compliances
- provide office space
- help with hotels, travel and food.

# The assessment process

Whatever certification body you choose, the assessment process will follow a similar pattern, with any differences being in terminology rather than content.

## *Document review*

The assessor's first job is to look at your quality management manual. This is where all the hard work you did for your internal desktop check will come into its own. The assessor will look hard to make sure that your manual either contains, or contains references to, all the documentation you need to meet the requirements of the ISO9000 standard. If you've missed something, the assessor will put the assessment process on hold until you have put the problem right.

The assessor will be happy to discuss with you any particular developments in your organisation which you are planning, or which have just begun, but which are not yet fully covered by procedures. For example, you may be thinking of installing a computer system, which will mean changing a lot of your procedures in the near future. The assessor will understand that your business can't stand still for the assessment process, so discuss your plans and agree how you will handle the change.

## Assessment

Assessment is the actual external audit process. It consists of an independent observer checking to see that what you say you do is what you actually do. Assessors will use the techniques which will be familiar to you from your internal auditing procedures: they will question, check and observe (see Figure 39).

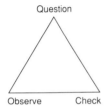

**Figure 39** *The audit triangle*

Assessors will look at all your documentation: your procedures, checklists and quality records. Assessors can follow functions, or cut across them. And as they question you, they will assume (nothing personal) that you are lying. This is where the checking part of the audit triangle comes in. The assessor will check procedures by looking at your quality management records, as specified in the quality management manual. If there isn't a record of something when there should be, the assessor will assume that the procedure hasn't taken place. Other procedures can be checked by observation, by noticing if the paperwork is where it should be, if date stamps are being used, if the filing is up to date, whether the stores area is in a mess, or the drawing office looks as if World War III has started. Remember nevertheless that assessors will probably be familiar with the way your industry works and with what is considered as normal for it. They won't expect clean room discipline in a general welding shop, just some kind of appropriate control.

## Report and recommendations

Throughout the assessment visit, the assessor will make careful notes and then report back on:

● major non-compliances or discrepancies

● minor non-compliances or discrepancies

● observations.

## Major non-compliances or discrepancies

Major non-compliances happen when part of the standard has not been implemented, or when there is an important system in your business which has not been documented in your quality management manual. When a major non-compliance is discovered it shows that you aren't formally in control of this part of the quality management system, and so the assessor will probably stop the assessment.

There are no clear figures published on companies who fail outright at assessment. Anecdotal figures suggest that this is less than 5 per cent.

## Minor non-compliances or discrepancies

Minor non-compliances are when the assessor finds small discrepancies between what you are doing and what the quality management manual says you do. For example, the assessor may find one or two examples of documents which are not properly controlled — this is a very common cause of minor non-compliance.

At assessment it is almost inevitable that minor non-compliances will be found — 10, 20 or sometimes more, depending on the size and complexity of your organisation. Don't be too despondent. As long as there are no major non-compliances, the assessment process will continue.

## Observations

Observations are similar to minor non-compliances. They are examples of really quite small-scale problems which don't affect how the system operates as a whole, but which suggests that the discipline of the organisation could be tightened up. The assessment process won't stop because of them.

## The closing meeting

At the end of the assessment visit, the assessors will hold what is known as a closing meeting with senior management to:

- give a verbal report of what they've found

- tell you what their recommendation for registration is going to be.

Unless you receive an unconditional recommendation for registration — which is really comparatively rare — or you have failed outright — which is an unlikely outcome at this stage — the assessor will give you a conditional recommendation for registration. You now have to put all the discrepancies right.

### Corrective action

At the closing meeting the assessor will have outlined the conditions of your registration, what you have to do to put things right. This information will now be confirmed in a written report. You might only have to correct some details of your procedures, which you can do by post, or the assessor may wish to visit you again within an agreed timescale.

This process tests the ability of your organisation to understand its own system and to correct any discrepancies using the proper methods. In a sense the assessor is testing your ability to implement and control changes to your system, which from their point of view is all important in the long term. After all, you may have employed an outsider to design and implement your system without actually being able to update the quality management manual yourself.

### Approval and registration to ISO9000

This protracted process means that it often seems as if there is no clear point at which you can pop the champagne corks and say that the project is finished. Meanwhile, pressure for a result will be building up from a number of sources:

- from the MD, who wants to tell the chairman that registration has been achieved, but can only say it has been granted conditionally

- from the sales director, who wants to tell your major clients, but who strictly speaking must wait until registration is confirmed

- from the marketing manager who wants to use the registered firms logo on your letterhead, your business cards, your sales literature, and your lorries and flags

- from the quality manager, who wants to take a well-deserved break, but who has to oversee corrective action.

Be patient and let the process take its course. You will get your registered firms logo and your very own registration number in the end. Make sure that you talk to your certification body about using the logo, by the way, before you print the stationery or use it in any other way. There are rules which govern what you can do, and expensive mistakes have been made.

And don't miss the publicity opportunities that registration will give you. Ask your certification body if they want to be involved.

## Surveillance visits

When the champagne bottles have been put away in the recycling bin and it's back to business as usual, the challenge, for you and for the certification body, is to make sure that the standard of conformance you achieved on assessment day is maintained. Backsliding after assessment day is a well-known phenomenon in the quality management world: it's hard to maintain the momentum after the excitement of the assessment process.

In order to check that you do maintain it, your assessor will visit you from time to time. There is a folk wisdom about these visits, which says that they can happen at any time and are unannounced. Just as you reach for your yellow stickies, the hand of the assessor will land on your shoulder. This model owes more to our in-built sense of guilt than to reality, however. In practice assessors do tell you when they are coming, if only so that you can keep time free for the inspection. And actually, a spot check shouldn't tell them anything that your quality management records won't. Conformance to the standard isn't an illusion you can put together for a day. It must have a visible impact on everything that you do, every day.

If the assessor finds examples of non-conformance during one of these post-assessment visits, you will be given a chance to put things right and a revisit will take place.

# Maintaining and developing the quality management manual

In your efforts to keep up a high level of conformance to the quality management manual, don't make the mistake we mentioned at the beginning of this chapter of coming to believe that the quality management manual is written on tablets of stone. It isn't, and furthermore it shouldn't be. There will be pressures for change from both inside and outside your organisation, to which your quality management manual must be responsive.

## Pressures for change

There can be very few industries left now which do not face what seems to be an almost constant pressure for change, both because of the world recession and because of the changing nature of markets. Survival in these conditions depends on the ability of the organisation to pick up signals quickly and to react with changes to policy and procedures. These changes may be myriad:

▲ We don't go into detail about change management issues in this book. If you are facing major change in your organisation, you should consult a textbook on the management of change.

many are likely to have an impact on your quality management manual.

For example, let's say that sales worldwide have slumped for one of the large multinationals. The company decides to separate out responsibility for different areas, so that poorly performing areas can be identified more quickly, and the management of more promising areas can be more responsive and maximise its opportunities.

These changes will be signalled clearly in the quality management manual by corresponding changes to:

- the organisation chart

- job roles and responsibilities

- reporting and control procedures.

So, far from representing a fixed system which inhibits change, the quality management manual should be seen and used as a way of defining and controlling the change processes which will inevitably take place over time.

There is clear evidence from organisations undergoing reorganisation that a quality management system which has been established for two or three years is a valuable tool in the change process.

### Mechanisms for change

There are dynamic mechanisms built into the ISO9000 quality management system to make sure that your quality management system does develop over time (see Figure 40). These mechanisms are:

**Figure 40** *Mechanisms for change in ISO9000*

- quality records
- audit
- corrective action
- management review.

## Quality records

Quality records are the deliverables from the quality management system. They make very interesting reading for management, since they provide a window through which any inefficiencies, any recurring problems or any unexpected developments in the business can be clearly seen. Management can then respond with appropriate and timely changes to procedures to put right the problems which have been highlighted.

In the case study at the end of the chapter, the organisation has realised the implications of ISO9000 for change and designed an elegant and very effective mechanism to:

- collect data
- analyse its significance
- pass it on to the policy-making levels of the company in a digestible form
- decide policy
- act on the policy, by updating the processes of the business.

## Audit

The principle behind audit is not just one of establishing conformance, although clearly an audit will tell you whether or not procedures are being followed. There is also an element of evaluation, of asking why there is non-conformance, of finding out whether the procedures work for people, or whether they are frankly a nuisance. As auditing becomes a familiar part of your management routine, your internal auditors should become increasingly sensitive to the nature of what people are saying and how to interpret it.

Sometimes complaints about the quality management system will be unwarranted, but others will be quite valid. Especially when the quality management system is in its infancy, you will find that some procedures don't work, or that there are mistakes, or that the system needs to change to keep up with technology.

Auditing very often picks up problems with duplicated work, for example. If people are asked to do the same thing twice in different ways, they probably won't bother. This is not so much a problem of conformance as of system design.

Auditing can also pick up problems with resources: perhaps people don't have enough time to fill in the paperwork, or follow consultation procedures, or whatever it is they aren't doing. If resources are finite, perhaps the procedures need to be more realistic.

Let's look at the case study at the end of the chapter. This organisation had 200 people trained in general audit methods, and a permanent core of 50–60 trained auditors. So if there was a problem, an audit team from the appropriate function would look at the problem and resolve it with the line manager.

If a line manager had a problem, their reaction would be to say: I've got a systems problem. Can you get an audit team to look at it for me?

In this organisation the link between ISO9000 and the management of change was very strong.

## Corrective action

The corrective action mechanism is like the help button on the computer, or perhaps the communication cord on a train. It's there to deal with problems and emergencies, when things clearly aren't going well. A good corrective action system should collect and collate information about problems and come up with solutions quickly in the form of amended procedures.

A word of warning though: the corrective action mechanism won't be able to deal with everything that comes up on a day-to-day basis. People should be encouraged to solve these problems on their own, and save the corrective action mechanism for significant changes to the system. Used in this way, it will allow you to investigate and resolve potentially disruptive problems.

## Management review

Management review is where the chief executive, who signed the quality policy statement, reviews the quality management system. This usually happens at a board meeting which will have an agreed agenda and formal minutes. The management review looks particularly at whether or not the quality management system is achieving the level of strategic importance it should.

# Change control procedures

To make changes to the quality management manual, you need to have agreed change control procedures. Any procedure should make sure that there is a dated record of:

- what exactly the change is

- who is authorising the change. You should severely limit the number of people who can authorise any changes — preferably to the project manager

- what issue of the quality management manual the change is to be made to

- what section or procedure of the quality management manual will be affected.

Strictly speaking, all copies of the manual should be updated every time a change is authorised. And if your manual is on a word processor, you could actually do that.

However, in practice you don't have to prepare a new issue for every small-scale adjustment which may result from an audit report or from a management review. Make sure that all authorised changes are recorded on one central copy of the quality management manual and on a change control list, and tell all the people who need to know about them what the changes are. Then, when there are a reasonable number of changes, or when you have reached a convenient point in time such as the year-end, you can reissue the quality management manual.

It may be that the changes you want to make only affect one particular section. In that case, you might want to reissue that section only. This is a useful compromise which enables you to keep the manual up to date without incurring the cost and bother of a full-scale reissue.

If there are major changes to be made, of course, you should prepare the new issue as quickly as you can, and institute a training programme as you did to introduce the quality management manual the first time round.

## *Recalling old issues*

Your circulation list tells you who has a copy of each issue of the quality management manual and therefore who will need to have a new one. However, not everyone on the circulation list needs a controlled copy. Some of the quality management manuals will have been distributed externally — to your quality management consultant, perhaps. These copies don't need to be updated, unless by request.

Everyone who does need to have a controlled copy must give back the old one when a reissue, in whole or in part, is due. This rule can be quite difficult to enforce, because people lose them. Or rather they don't really lose them, but temporarily misplace them when the reissue comes out, then find them again and start using the wrong copy when no one is watching. Suddenly there are two versions in use.

Some large organisations are so worried by this problem that they require all their employees to know at all times where their copy of the quality management manual is. This might seem extreme, but it represents a useful discipline.

We talked before about having a role for document police when the quality management system is being implemented. There is a further role for your squad at reissue time, to make sure that all controlled copies are found and replaced.

## Developing the quality management manual

Finally, keep thinking creatively about how you can improve and develop the way the quality management manual is presented. All the way through this book we have emphasised the importance of the style and presentation of the quality management manual, as well as its content. As the quality management manual goes into circulation, you will have ample opportunity to find out if you have succeeded in creating an attractive, usable document, or if you have not managed to get beyond the barriers of jargon, unclear language and poorly executed, unstructured design.

You can collect feedback informally by asking people what they think, or you can devise a more systematic kind of approach. This would involve things like:

- testing access structures. Ask people to find things, and see how long it takes them

- testing comprehensibility. Pick out a few of your more long-winded procedures and ask people what they mean

- surveying impressions, possibly with a questionnaire.

Based on the responses you receive, you can then start to experiment with different structures and formats.

Some companies are beginning at last to move away from the traditional quality management manual format — worthy but dull and rather difficult. However attention is often focused on rather superficial changes such as the use of colour, or size of format, rather than really addressing deep-rooted questions of structure and meaning. The average quality management manual is still quite difficult to navigate.

As part of your policy of continuous improvement, why not resolve to move ahead of the field and develop a quality management manual which not only reflects your business accurately and responsively, but which also reflects the level of sophistication in communications that people have grown to expect. Modern technology means that doing that isn't really very much more expensive than anything else. It will be a good investment and give you that most logical of products, a good quality management manual.

## Case Study

### Belton Storage Systems Ltd – Reviewing and Adding Value to the Quality Management Manual

This case study consists of papers and charts from Belton Storage Systems Ltd's management review report for 1990. It gives a snapshot of how one company is using its quality records in a dynamic way to analyse the business, particularly from the customer's perspective, and to make sure its procedures are constantly improved and updated through the change request procedures. These changes to procedure will then find their way into the company's quality management manual.

## Management Review — quality report for BS5750

**Belton Storage Systems Ltd**
**1990**

### Contents

1.  Assessor's visits and discrepancies
2.  Procedures manual status
3.  Change requests
4.  Corrective action and customer complaints
5.  Audit analysis and review

### 1 Assessor's visits and discrepancies

1.1  2 August 1989. Location: Birmingham
Routine assessment. Two minor discrepancies raised — both cleared.

1.2  18 October 1989. Location: Birmingham.
Routine assessment. Three minor discrepancies raised — two cleared, one disputed. (Assessor accepted explanation.)

1.3  2 February 1990. Location: Nottingham — installation site. No discrepancies.

1.4  15 May 1990. Location: Birmingham
Routine assessment. Four minor discrepancies raised — all cleared.

**Note:** Informal communication to assessor on quality of auditing at this assessment. We felt that it was sub-standard.

1.5  2 August 1990. Location: Primrose Hill regional office.
Two discrepancies raised — both cleared.

**Note**

*Quality Assessment Schedule QAS/3204/274 Issue 2 relating to static racking and shelving systems.*
This is an additional set of industry standards developed by the BSi which must be adhered to whilst still satisfying the requirements of BS5750.

All changes in the QAS have been included in the company procedures.

## 2 Procedure manual status

2.1 Procedures issued or re-issued since the last management review

| Number | Name | Issue | Date |
|---|---|---|---|
| 200 | Procedures manual | 6 | 7.6.90 |
| 310 | Contract review – quotes | Not reissued | |
| 311 | Orders | 3 | 4.1.90 |
| 320 | Product development | 3 | 3.5.90 |
| | | 4 | 4.9.90 |
| 330 | Production engineering | 4 | 18.9.90 |
| 340 | Process engineering | Not reissued | |
| 351 | Coil receipt | 3 | 29.5.90 |
| | | 4 | 27.6.90 |
| 370 | Applications engineering | 4 | 13.3.90 |
| 380 | Marketing | Not reissued | |
| 391 | Organisation and authority levels | 2 | 12.2.90 |
| | | 3 | 20.3.90 |
| | | 4 | 25.6.90 |
| 393 | Warehouse | Not issued* | |
| 394 | Perpetual inventory | Not issued* | |

* Procedures not issued or current, due to constant development in these areas.

2.2 Procedures being revised, introduced or consolidated

| Number | Name | Action | Due date |
|--------|------|--------|----------|
| 100 | Policy manual | Revise | Oct 90 |
| 200 | Procedures manual | Revise | Oct 90 |
| 357 | Office systems manual | Introduce | Oct 90 |
| 350 | Apple component take-off | Introduce | Oct 90 |

### 3 Change requests

Figures are obtained from data collected between 4.7.89 and 1.10.90

| | |
|---|---|
| Change requests raised: | 593 |
| Change requests actioned: | 483 |
| Current status: | 110 outstanding |
| | 30 within action period (1 month of raising) |

*Breakdown*

| **Generating department** | **Actioning department** |
|---------------------------|--------------------------|
| Accounts 200 | Production engineering 386 |
| Office systems 72 | Product development 105 |
| Production engineering 68 | Office systems 36 |
| Production control 70 | Computer services 38 |
| Quality assurance 45 | Purchasing 31 |
| Manufacturing 57 | Applications engineering 29 |
| Purchasing 21 | Quality assurance 28 |
| Works engineering 15 | Marketing 15 |
| Applications engineering 13 | Stores department 15 |
| Stores department 17 | Sales 14 |
| Other 15 | Other 38 |
| **Total 593** | **735** |

**Note:** One change request may result in multiple changes involving several departments.

## 4 Corrective actions and customer complaints: Type 1 orders

**Table 1:** Number of queries received per product by sales region
Period: Week 28 1989 to week 39 1990

*Sales regions*

| Products | SR | NR | SC | Dan | Osl | Irl | Total |
|---|---|---|---|---|---|---|---|
| Fastfit | 58 | 98 | 0 | 20 | 0 | 52 | 228 |
| Office | 147 | 86 | 1 | 9 | 0 | 26 | 269 |
| Demountable | 50 | 36 | 0 | 1 | 0 | 12 | 99 |
| Stores | 10 | 24 | 1 | 1 | 0 | 3 | 39 |
| Small systems | 58 | 42 | 0 | 5 | 0 | 15 | 120 |
| Archive | 0 | 0 | 0 | 0 | 305 | 2 | 307 |
| Furniture | 9 | 0 | 0 | 0 | 23 | 1 | 33 |
| Other | 73 | 31 | 0 | 1 | 60 | 0 | 165 |
| **Total** | **405** | **317** | **2** | **37** | **388** | **111** | **1260** |

**Table 2:** Number of types of problem per product
Period: Week 28 1989 to week 39 1990

*Products*

| Problems | SL | I | A | SD | SP | Par | PID | Oth | Total |
|---|---|---|---|---|---|---|---|---|---|
| Short delivery | 96 | 152 | 53 | 8 | 40 | 4 | 2 | 65 | 420 |
| Damaged | 26 | 43 | 8 | 1 | 0 | 5 | 57 | 2 | 142 |
| Wrong goods | 37 | 70 | 21 | 6 | 0 | 12 | 89 | 14 | 249 |
| Late | 14 | 8 | 13 | 7 | 4 | 9 | 8 | 2 | 65 |
| Wrong discount | 32 | 17 | 12 | 3 | 1 | 13 | 35 | 38 | 151 |
| Cancellation | 3 | 3 | 0 | 0 | 0 | 3 | 1 | 2 | 12 |
| Early delivery | 1 | 2 | 0 | 0 | 0 | 1 | 0 | 0 | 4 |
| Balance prob | 5 | 7 | 1 | 1 | 1 | 35 | 1 | 6 | 57 |
| **Total** | **214** | **302** | **108** | **26** | **46** | **82** | **193** | **129** | **1100** |

*Project management*

### *Type 2 orders*

Figures year to date from 1.1.1990
Number of enquiries raised:     65
Number actioned:                27

**Table 3:** Number of enquiries per generating department

| Department | Enquiries |
|---|---|
| Office systems | 8 |
| Sales | 27 |
| Marketing | 5 |
| Quality assurance | 6 |
| Contracts | 18 |
| Production | 1 |

**Table 4:** Number of enquiries dealt with per actioning department

**Note:** Corrective actions may result in multiple actions

| Actioning department | Enquiries |
|---|---|
| Production engineering | 15 |
| Quality assurance | 21 |
| Development | 1 |
| Sales | 1 |
| Manufacturing | 15 |
| Purchasing | 11 |
| Distribution | 8 |
| Applications engineering | 2 |
| Accounts | 1 |

# Appendix

ANYNAME CONSULTANTS

# Quality Procedures Manual

**1** Business management

**2** Assignment management

**3** Personnel management

**4** Company administration

**5** Quality assurance

| | | | |
|---|---|---|---|
| Issue number: 1 | Authorised by: | Copy number: | |
| Date: 5.12.93 | | Issued to: | |

# 2 Assignment management

2.1   Commissioning

2.2   Execution

2.3   Completion

2.4   Follow-up

2.5   Exceptional procedures

*Anyname Consultants*
Quality procedures manual

*Version control*
Issue number: 1
Date: 5.12.93
Section: 2.0    Page: 1 of 1

**2.0**

## 2.1 Commissioning

### Purpose

To ensure that client enquiries are managed responsively.

### Scope

The commissioning stage of a project starts with the initial contact with a prospective client about a particular project, and includes the company's proposal for the project, and its outcome.

These procedures cover all enquiries.

### Responsibilties

Directors are responsible for client contact at the commissioning stage. They may nominate others to act as proposal managers for particular bids.

### References

Wordprocessor software and manual
E-mail software and manual
C3      Address book
R2.2    Proposal guidelines
R2.3    Quotation guidelines
R2.4    Proposal checklist

### Forms

F2.1    Initial Contact Report
F2.2    Proposal Manager Briefing
F2.3    Client Contact Report
F2.4    Proposal Outcome Report
F3.5    Sign-off Form

*Anyname Consultants*
Quality procedures manual

*Version control*
Issue number: 1
Date: 5.12.93
Section: 2.1 Page: 1 of 3

**2.1.1**

## 2.1    Commissioning time-line

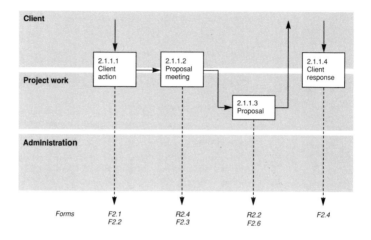

*Anyname Consultants*
Quality procedures manual

*Version control*
Issue number: 1
Date: 5.12.93
Section: 2.1 Page: 2 of 3

**2.1.2**

### 2.1.1 Commissioning procedures

#### 2.1.1.1 Client action

Client enquiries are made by post, phone or fax and are referred to a director. Anyone, including a director, who takes a client enquiry, records the details on an Initial Contact Report (F2.1) and copies it to all directors.

If the company does not already have details of the prospective client, the person who took the enquiry enters it in the address book.

The directors discuss the potential project, and appoint a proposal manager. This is recorded on a Proposal Manager Briefing Form (F2.2).

#### 2.1.1.2 Proposal meeting

The proposal manager may have a further discussion with the client about the job, and what the proposal should cover. The proposal manager uses the Proposal Checklist (R2.4) as a brief for this discussion. A summary of this meeting or discussion is recorded on a Client Contact Report (F2.3).

The proposal manager opens a proposal file to keep records of the commissioning stage, including letters, tender documents or print-outs of E-mail forms.

#### 2.1.1.3 Proposal

The proposal is prepared using the Proposal Guidelines (R2.2) for style, content and presentation. The proposal is proof-read for errors and signed off by a director on a Sign-off Form (F2.6))

Three copies are made for:
1 the client
2 the proposal file
3 the Business Manager.

#### 2.1.1.4 Client response

The proposal manager records the outcome of the proposal on a Proposal Outcome Report (F2.4). This is sent to the directors and a copy filed in the proposal file.

If the proposal is *successful,* the Office Manager is asked to allocate a job number and sends the number to the proposal manager. The project then moves to the Execution phase (section 2.2 of this manual).

If the proposal is *unsuccessful,* the proposal manager include a debriefing note to go in the Proposal Outcome Report. If the client has not already indicated a reason for the outcome, they should be contacted to probe for the reason.

*Anyname Consultants*
Quality procedures manual

*Version control*
Issue number: 1
Date: 5.12.93
Section: 2.1 Page: 2 of 3

**2.1.3**

# Index